Begin with Rock, End with Water

MERCER
UNIVERSITY PRESS

Endowed by
TOM WATSON BROWN
and
THE WATSON-BROWN FOUNDATION, INC.

BEGIN WITH ROCK, END WITH WATER

Essays

John Lane

MERCER UNIVERSITY PRESS
MACON, GEORGIA

MUP/ P451

© 2012 Mercer University Press
1400 Coleman Avenue
Macon, Georgia 31207

First Edition

Books published by Mercer University Press are printed on acid-free paper that meets the requirements of the American National Standard for Information Sciences—Permanence of Paper for Printed Library Materials.

Mercer University Press is a member of Green Press Initiative (greenpressinitiative.org), a nonprofit organization working to help publishers and printers increase their use of recycled paper and decrease their use of fiber derived from endangered forests. This book is printed on recycled paper.

ISBN   978-0-88146-384-2

Cataloging-in-Publication Data is available from the Library of Congress

CONTENTS

Acknowledgments

"Youghiogheny" appeared in *Adventure America* (National Geographic Books, 2002) under the title "River Wild;" "On the Chattooga" appeared in *The South Carolina Review* (Clemson University); "ReGenesis" appeared in *Watershed Journal* (Brown University); "Sardis" appeared in *Prairie Schooner* (University of Nebraska); "Lake Conestee" appeared in *A Voice for the Earth: American Writers Respond to the Earth Charter* edited by Peter Blaze Corcoran and A. James Wahlpart (University of Georgia Press, 2008); "Coachwhip" appeared in *Ecotones* (University of North Carolina-Wilmington); A shorted version of "Wild Piedmont" appeared in *Heartstone* (Warren Wilson College); "Circumambulation" appeared in *ISLE* (University of Nevada-Reno); "Sols Creek Falls" appeared in *The Smoky Mountain News* (Waynesville, North Carolina) and in *High Vista: An Anthology of Nature Writing from Western North Carolina and the Great Smokey Mountains, Volume II 1900-2009,* edited by George Ellison (Natural History Press, Charleston, SC 2011); "Carnival against Capitalism" appeared in *Creative Loafing* (Greenville, South Carolina, 1999); "A Hole in Time" first appeared in *Terrain.org*(online, 2010).

Many thanks to those who have accompanied me on these excursions into "nearby nature" of my own backyard and the wilder place further away—Randy Riddle, Franklin Burroughs, Ellen Goldey, Dave Hargett, Gerald Thurmond, G. R. Davis, Thomas Pierce, Padgett Powell, Dixon Bynum, Wes Cooler, Butch Clay, David Scott, Ab Abercrombie, and Betsy Scott. As always, I'm indebted to Deno Trakas, Beth Ely, both good readers who always enjoy the journey no matter where I take them, and especially to Betsy, Rob, and Russell, who are with me always and make it all possible. Also, thanks to periodical editors Scott McCloud at *The Smoky Mountain News,*

Wayne Chapman at *The South Carolina Review,* Margo Flood at *Heartstone,* David Gessner at *Ecotone.* Many thanks also to Gree and all the folks at the National Geographic Society for trusting me to paddle a wild river from top to bottom on their dime.

Finally, for support of time and money while writing several of these pieces I'd like to thank Wofford College, the Ossabaw Foundation, The National Science Foundation, and The Spartanburg Water & Sewer District. Thanks also to Marc Jolley and the staff at Mercer University Press.

The title of the collection is taken from Theodore Roethke's poem, "Bring the Day!" from *Praise to the End.*

Also by John Lane

Prose
Weed Time
Waist Deep in Black Water
Chattooga
Circling Home
The Best of the Kudzu Telegraph
My Paddle to the Sea

Poetry
Quarries
As the World Around us Sleeps
Against Information & Other Poems
The Dead Father Poems
Noble Trees
Abandoned Quarry: New & Selected Poems

Edited
Hub City Anthology
Hub City Christmas
The Woods Stretched for Miles

Begin with Rock, End with Water

I

A little too abstract, a little too wise,
It is time for us to kiss the earth again,
It is time to let the leaves rain from the skies,
Let the rich life run to the roots again.
—Robinson Jeffers from "Return"

SARDIS

Easter Sunday and it's windy and cold for April in the Deep South. To make matters worse, squall lines have been blowing up from the Gulf all morning, hanging tattered clouds so low and thick they look like the soaked inside of a cotton bale. I'm on a three-day book tour—first Memphis, then Jackson and Oxford, Mississippi—for *Chattooga*, a narrative about the river made famous in part by Southern writer James Dickey. It hasn't really been a triumphant tour. On Saturday afternoon in Memphis, the Davis-Kidd chain store where I was scheduled to sign forgot to order *Chattooga* from the publisher. I stood around for twenty minutes while an embarrassed clerk searched for two copies of the book the computer said they had somewhere in the store. My one other stop in Memphis that evening was at an independent bookstore where, upon arrival, I discovered they'd closed early for Easter. There was a small handwritten sign in the window next to a nice pile of my unsigned *Chattooga* that said, "Gone Fishin'." I am still hopeful concerning stops in Jackson and Oxford on Monday. The bookstores there—Lemuria in Jackson and Square Books in Oxford—are legendary in their hospitality to writers. Other writer friends who'd done this very tour told me I would not be disappointed with either.

Since I'm so close, I've told my Mississippi buddy Dixon Bynum I want to salve my tour wounds by paddling some of what's left of the river bottom of Faulkner's "Big Woods." Dixon has set up a 6-mile, half-day paddle downstream from the Sardis dam, on what little free-flow is left of the Little Tallahatchie River, which becomes the Tallahatchie 30 miles downstream after its confluence with the Coldwater River. It's no wilderness, but it will give me a window cracked open on what Faulkner calls the "tall and endless" woods.

William Faulkner made up a mythical Mississippi county with the unpronounceable Native-American name of Yoknapatawpha, and James Dickey did the same with a North Georgia river called the Cahulawassee. Both mythical places have lived in my imagination parallel to real places. Both landscapes—the real and the imagined—have their appeal.

Is it Faulkner's Big Woods drowned under Sardis Lake? Not really. The big bottom of "The Bear" isn't any more a real place than Jefferson or Frenchman's Bend or the old Sutpen's Hundred. Dixon assures me though that southwest of here is where the real Faulkner is known to have hunted and camped along a real Mississippi river, and surely he used his experience in the Little Tallahatchie river bottom to create "The Bear" and several other stories. "Write what you know," that's what we tell our students in creative writing classes.

I've driven out of Memphis south on I-55 parallel to the Big Muddy. After an hour, I get on Highway 315, approach, and cross the Sardis Dam—a vast mowed greensward of earthen construction so long (over a half-mile) that the Corps of Engineers has made a park out of the base of it with football and soccer fields. I cruise over the causeway and see that the dull brown lake's on one side humming with motorboats. The recreation space is down slope on the other. The whole complex is like a snapshot of twentieth-century engineering logic—drown something dynamic and wild like the Little Tallahatchie River, offer car camping, fishing, boating, chalk off a playing field or two, and call it "green space."

In the Deep South, there's little natural about a big lake. The terrain of Mississippi remained glacier-free in the Pleistocene and, if not manipulated, the local water does what it's done for hundreds of thousands of years, eventually finding its way to the Gulf of Mexico. Even the ox-bow lakes on the Mississippi are ephemeral in geologic time, cut-off meanders filling in every few thousand years to form bogs, dells, swamps, and finally covered with thick riparian forest of cypress and tupelo. Check out any North Mississippi lake holding enough water to drop a ski boat in, and at the outlet you'll find a water control system of some sort, a low earthen levee cutting across the stream flow, a shallow concrete dam, or a bigger dam made of earth, rock, masonry, concrete, or some combination of the above.

I don't like dams, but I have to admit I'm probably in the minority. Impoundments have been around awhile. Some say as little as 1 percent of all the water on the planet is available to us, not salty or frozen in glaciers, and that tiny bit of water is often not in the right place for us humans to do with it what we need for survival—drink it or use it to ensure ample crops. Human engineering of water flow dates back to the Egyptians who built irrigation systems. When, in Monty Python's *Life of Brian*, a member of one of the numerous liberation fronts during the time of Christ answers the rhetorical question, "What have the Romans ever done for us?" he only needs one word—"Aqueducts." It even gets a laugh out of me.

Who could dislike aqueducts? Architecturally, an aqueduct looks more like a Roman temple than does Sardis Dam. Their elegant arches show some classic sensitivity to place and space. They survive as ruins and in some rare instances still do what they were designed to do 2,000 years ago—move water from a place of abundance to one of scarcity.

Once human beings start engineering, it's hard to stop. There's a direct line from a marble dam built in India in 1660 for water impoundment and crop cultivation to the huge contemporary hydro projects like China's Three Gorges Dam, trapping whole river drainages under its vastness. If you're a hydraulic engineer with a hammer in your hand—in this case with enough knowledge to build a dam—it doesn't take much to see the dams plugging the planet's vast river systems as your nails.

I know my feelings of disdain for reservoirs flow from a place of Western economic privilege. China argues they need the Three Gorges Dam for hydro-power to fuel their future and pull billions out of poverty. I trust when I turn on my tap at home in South Carolina that water will flow forth. When I eat a salad, I know some engineer has long ago guaranteed the lettuce will be irrigated in a semi-arid California field. But it isn't these human uses that I seriously question. It's our need for impoundments like Sardis; it's the desire so many Corps of Engineers impoundments in the South articulate—rivers drowned for flood control, recreation, and aesthetics.

Construction on Lake Sardis began in 1936 as flood control for the southern Mississippi River Valley after the great flood of 1927 had swamped the whole vast flood plain of the Mississippi Delta from the bluffs in Arkansas to the bluffs in Mississippi, a distance of more than fifty miles. In the wake of that famous flood, the Corps of Engineers built these now familiar dams, floodways, spillways, levees; they did channel stabilization and channel mapping. They cut meanders on the Mississippi, shortening the river's route to the Gulf by 152 miles. They tamed the river and any tributary that might offer trouble again.

In the 1930s, there was little doubt that "flood control" was desirable. Most years people die from floods, and property is lost. Who could argue that if engineering floods is possible we should not do it? Recently though, "control" has been substituted for "management," and the prevailing wisdom (even in the Corps of Engineers) is that bigger dams make for greater damage once a big flood does come. Is it possible that the era of large dams for flood control and development has drawn to a close?

A few hours alone in a rental car have given me way too much time to think about all this and made me way too cynical about taming rivers and landscapes with reservoirs like Sardis. The catchphrase "God would have done it, if he had the money—" rings throughout the South about the federal agency's makeover of the world in its own image. As I drove out of Memphis, I pondered the South fallen off from what I long for as an old romantic and preservationist anarchist. I mourn all the species lost to development, the logging, the rude run-off from paving the continent, the engineered rivers in the Mississippi River Valley and the manmade lakes holding back the waters bound for the Gulf.

Though the name of Lake Sardis slightly echoes one of Faulkner's most famous families, Sartoris, I don't think the 1950 recipient of the Nobel Prize would recognize much of his native county now. My friend Dixon says Faulkner knew Lake Sardis and even opposed it at first. He wrote a letter to the Oxford paper articulating his views on what the Corps of Engineers called "progress." It's not hard to hear echoes of Faulkner's uneasy relationship with progress in the first few pages of "The Bear" from *Go Down, Moses*, first published in 1940, the year Sardis Lake's flood gates closed and water began to back up over the big bottom. In "The Bear," Faulkner describes the modern countryside around the bottom as "a corridor of wreckage and destruction" and compares progress moving through it with "the ruthless and irresistible deliberation of a locomotive, the shaggy tremendous shape." Dixon guesses that by the 1950s, Faulkner seemed to have made his peace with the lake. He often escaped from his increasing fan base by retreating to a houseboat named *Mingagery* he kept at the Sardis marina. As one biographer says, "He spent a good deal of time on his boat, sulking, avoiding contact with the world." There's even a famous picture of the Nobel Prize-winner plying the waters of Sardis Lake on a sailboat he owned called the *Ring Dove*. As far as I know, there are no photos of Faulkner in a canoe floating downstream toward Batesville on the Little Tallahatchie.

What would William Faulkner make of the interstate highway system that brought me here or the campers parked at the foot of the 15,000-foot-long dam? Driving in, I see a little slice of what's left of Faulkner's countryside—dogwoods in bloom, abandoned farmsteads, closed cinderblock country stores only a few generations removed from one like Flem Snopes might have run, a stray black dog working the roadside for whatever scraps he can find, a vista out over newly plowed fields of the hill country around Oxford, and the dark silence of a far way hardwood tree line in the distance. But there is also the new rural South— on the way down, signs advertising Mallard Pointe Golf Course halfway to Memphis, and a convenience store called the Dam Store anchoring the turn-off for the resort on the lake's western shore. As I pull into the Sardis Dam parking lot, I think how for Faulkner the past pools in the present, wetting down the future, and never evaporates. From reading his novels and stories, I know nothing's purely downstream in Faulkner's world.

I've arrived a little early, so I park the rental car and wait for Dixon's pickup. He's told me to look for a crew-cab Toyota Tacoma, but it would be easy to spot the truck anyway because of his canoe. "By their racks, ye shall know them," said a bumper sticker I once saw on a paddler's car. I'm a little cold— dressed like a touring writer for the raw, wet, windy spring day. Though I know I'm going paddling, I haven't packed well. I thought in April a pair of shorts and a tee would do. Leaving the motel at 6:00 A.M. I slipped on all three dress shirts I'd brought and a wind shell, but it's still not cutting the wind and chill. While I wait, I walk down and look at the Sardis spillway to keep warm. It's wide open, booming—a massive plug of heaving Delta water from the impounded Little Tallahatchie River coming through every second. This chilly Easter morning locals fish the riprap banks. Just downstream a smaller, quiet lower lake spreads out, and three aluminum skiffs trawl down toward where the river flows out over a low-head dam. There's no shortage of reading material as I wait. A "posted limit" sign reminds anglers they are allowed seven black bass or crappie per day.

Soon I'm walking back up the ramp to the parking lot, and Dixon's truck pulls in, followed by another car, a Chevy truck with a camper top and canoe on top. When Dixon's window comes down, I hear birdcalls coming from the cab. We shake hands though and Dixon knows I'm a little confused by the whistles and chirps, and he explains that the bootleg birdcall tapes are a habit he picked up while he was writing his thesis at Mississippi on Audubon. "My wife nearly left me over these damn tapes," Dixon says. "I still don't know 'em all. Get in; we're gonna run the shuttle first."

When I'm in the warm cab and buckled in, Dixon nods back to the following Suburban and says he's brought a graduate-school friend, Greg Brown, along to paddle, says Greg is working on the prosody of English poetry. "A strange passion in Faulkner country," I comment, and Dixon just laughs. "It's a big department."

Dixon takes off, and we head back down Highway 315 to a cut-through gravel road that parallels the river five miles downstream to the next bridge where we'll drop Greg's car. Dixon says we'll stop along the way and walk a boardwalk through a tupelo swamp, something he thinks I should see if I'm going to visit Mississippi searching for Faulkner's big bottom. Unlike me, Dixon's dressed for the weather. He's wearing two or three layers topped by a golden hunting jacket. He's got a ball cap to top off his head, blue jeans and worn-out L.L. Bean "duck boots" to protect his feet from the wet morning as we paddle. Pulling into the parking lot for the boardwalk Dixon explains how it's not predicted to climb above fifty today and will stay windy. "Raw spring day," is how he puts it, looking at my underdressed torso. "I've got a second paddling jacket. You're gonna need it."

Dixon, Greg, and I walk from the parking lot toward the boardwalk. The sun's out, and it's warmer. Greg's a friendly guy, dressed like Dixon for the weather. Dixon tells him I've commented on the oddness of a scholar of English poetry prosody in Faulkner Country, and Greg makes it clear that while not studying English poetry he gets in as many canoe expeditions as possible, day-trips and overnights, the rhythm of canoe paddling blending nicely with all the conventional rhythms of poetry. On the way in, Dixon says both he and Greg get to walk here more than they get to canoe. This boardwalk is only twenty minutes from Oxford and affords a nice escape from graduate school. He directs my attention to two large clusters of buckeye growing near the parking lot already boasting a showy display of red dangling blooms. I wish for a moment I had a concordance of all Mississippi writers so I could see ways they've used plants in their fiction. Is there anywhere in Faulkner where a character comments on buckeye blooming in the spring? Does Eudora Welty weave the buckeye into any story, or does a range map of her fiction leave the buckeye high on the bluffs above the river?

When we enter the swamp proper, Dixon points out tupelo leafing out in the marginal forest, and I know I'm in the Deep South. The rough buttressed trunks of the tupelo are dark grayish, still wet from the rain blowing through in waves this morning. Is this the remaining Mississippi equivalent of the mythic forest Faulkner found "somber, impenetrable" in "The Bear?"

We circle out on the wooden boardwalk to the middle of the swamp, and it terminates at two large observation platforms. Taking up the center of the swamp is a large beaver pond. I look around. Two great blue herons fish in the shallows just far enough away to stay undisturbed by our presence. A kingfisher cackles as we pause. Dixon has brought his field glasses and swivels them to his eyes and scans the distant tree line where he knows from his other visits here there is a beaver lodge.

"Look at that," Dixon says, in a moment or two, pointing toward the middle of the pond. With my bare eyes, I can see what looks like two muskrats on steroids that have risen out of the pond to frolic on a hummock of brush. "Nutria," Dixon says. "Two big ones. It looks like they are grooming each other." Dixon hands me the glasses, and I watch intently. They are not Old Ben, the bear of the big bottom, but the wild nutria will have to do for megafauna today. As I watch, Greg gives me a little natural history. The rodents—close kin to beavers and muskrats—were introduced to the Gulf states as a furbearer from South America in the early 1900s. They've worked inland from freshwater marsh to marsh for a hundred years, helped along the way by a storm surge or two. Herbivores, they eat pickerelweed, cattail, and arrowhead, and in the winter gnaw the bark from wetland hardwoods. Nutria have long yellow incisors like beaver and graze up to 25 percent of their body weight in a single day.

Dixon adds that they are not beloved wildlife in the Delta. They destroy wetlands with their voracious grazing of aquatic plants, and the young are sexually mature in only four months. If nutria is an indicator species for anything it's how quickly things can get out of control when we try to engineer natural systems for our own good. The nutria is sort of a dark twin to Faulkner's bear roaming the Big Bottom for generations in spite of, as Faulkner beautifully puts it, "man's puny gnawing at the immemorial flank" of the forest. Now we've gnawed practically everything away and sent in the mercenaries—the nutria, the Asian clams, the kudzu and the Japanese honeysuckle—to gobble up and colonize what's left.

On the drive down to the take-out bridge we pass still active farm fields, newly plowed. Dixon points out an old abandoned silo with "white power" scrawled in black paint across the curving concrete. As we pass closer I see it's also riddled with large caliber bullet holes. "Well, it's still Mississippi," Dixon says, laughing. The scene chills me a little though, a leftover from *Mississippi Burning*. Violence is always right here, in imagination, just below the surface in the countryside—bullet holes and racist slogans—and any protection from being an outsider drains away.

We drop Greg's truck at the take-out, transfer his boat, and drive back to the Sardis Dam. With gulls circling overhead and a two-foot dead gar, empty-eyed, bobbing at the water's edge, we put in at the boat ramp on the lower lake. Dixon and I push his fourteen-foot Old Town tandem out from shore as Greg steps in his Mad River Intrepid set up to paddle solo. A bass boat launches right as we do, and the local boys can't resist getting in a little shot at our mode of travel. "You boys might be needing a tow back," yells the Mississippi Bubba in camo bib overalls as we begin to stroke across the lake.

First 2 miles downstream, the Little Tallahatchie, set free from the Sardis impoundment, meanders through forested banks of what Dixon calls "the Corps land," and if I squint it's possible to imagine I'm paddling some primordial bend in an ancient Southern river. I ask Dixon where the Delta officially begins, and he repeats historian David Cohen's famous comment from 1935: "In the lobby of the Peabody Hotel in Memphis," then gives me the answer I'm looking for: "20 miles southwest, but ecologically, it's right here. This is a fringe Delta stream and it shares many of the Delta's characteristics— tupelo and other bottomland hardwoods, but it's also got the Northern Mississippi species like the dogwood."

I make a survey of the ecological zone we're passing through. The dogwoods Dixon has mentioned are blooming in the understory. Swallows work the surface of the river for insects. Then the trees disappear, and the vista opens up into newly plowed farmland, and the banks, upstream held in place by trees and understory vegetation, are now deeply eroded where the farmers have planted row crops right up to river's edge. "They all know about best management practices," Dixon says. "But they choose to ignore them."

For an hour or so, we talk about whatever is passing—a deer breaking through a thicket, great blue herons fishing in the shallows. Halfway down we take Greg's lead and follow him up a tributary creek. When we enter, it narrows down to ten feet, but we begin to see more birds in the denser cover— kingfishers, green herons, more great blues. Before we turn around, we even begin to see the distinctive flared trunks of some mature cypress.

As we float, Dixon talks about how much he loves a day on the river, any day. I ask if he's ever taken his canoe out on the Mississippi, and he recalls a race he'd been in, the only time he'd ever really paddled the big river in a canoe. He also talks about a long wild trip on the Pearl River in Southern Mississippi he and Greg have been planning—six days, all the way to the Gulf, from Jackson on down. He seemed to anticipate these canoe trips the way the narrator of "The Bear" anticipated the yearly journey into the Big Bottom to hunt. The Big Bottom might be gone, but the yearning to get out in the dense still exists.

We've soon left the little tributary, and we're back to the river proper and headed downstream. We stop for water and some crackers on the only gravel bar we've seen—all river sand everywhere else. Here, the water rushes over a beach of dull cobbles, not so much many colored as variations on a shade of brown, and Dixon mentions that Tallahatchie is a Native-American word that means either "river town" or "rock river." I pick one up the size of a baseball and feel the curve worn smooth by tumbling. The smoothness is a fossil of passing time. This chunk weathered or eroded out of an outcrop somewhere north of here and rolled along the river to end up at our feet.

Dixon says twenty miles southwest the Little Tallahatchie enters the Delta proper and begins its run over deep sediments laid down by thousands of years of Mississippi floods, the rich black alluvial soil where the blues grew alongside cypress, cotton, and soybeans. The Delta loam downstream birthed a culture, birthed a way of life, but the hill country we're floating through south of Lake Sardis did all right as well. It birthed Faulkner, an intellectual industry, birthed a place inhabited by stories, what historian Don H. Doyle calls "the most Southern of all places."

I'm out of place here, a native of the upper South plunged deep for a day in an unfamiliar landscape and topography. Though I can name a few trees, those on the riverside are still a little foreign, as is the weight of the air, the pitch of the horizon. If Doyle is right and Faulkner's Yoknapatawpha County, laid mythically on top of Dixon's real life Lafayette County, is the essential South, then I have a right to feel like I'm a visitor. I settle back to appreciate it. I look south with the flowing river. The sun falls in glittering slats across the surface. The water surges over the stones at the edge of the bed.

But soon it's time to come back to the river and its flow, step in the boats and let the current take us downstream. Knowing too much can tear you from the moment, can get you lost in ideas and speculation, and when you finally do look around you have to blink hard to get some focus. As we head downstream, I see the ridges are a quarter-mile distant from the channel here. In the old days, before flood control, the river took every inch of the space between the ridges in high flow. Now the Corps controls the river through the spillways at Sardis dam. I ask Dixon if he's ever seen the river high, and he says higher than this, but not much, not out in the fields laying down silt like it used to every spring. This makes me think about the river moving us downstream and the action of the ancient current. I remember how the river channel is almost completely absent from Faulkner's account of hunting in the Big Bottom. You know the river's there because it has to be, but McCaslin never describes it. McCaslin's attention is on the woods still thick and mysterious in the flood plain before the loggers take it down, not the river running through it.

But today we are canoeists, not hunters, and so we make our recreation in the river channel. For Faulkner, "The Bear" is a eulogy to a lost way of life, a time when once a year men retreated to the pure Mississippi wilderness to hunt for a month at a time living in a camp. We retreat with river running, paddling stretches of territory where it's possible to forget the university and the soccer fields and the spillways and the dams upstream. Outdoor recreation has become our passage, our deliverance from town life.

As we float along, Dixon gets quiet, listening for birds he can recall from his Audubon tapes, and it gives me time to conjure some half-baked theory about when Faulkner wrote and how it was like a last big wild river being dammed. All those Mississippi stories from Chickasaw and Choctaw times, forward flowing around and through him, finally ending up in over a dozen novels and a hundred short stories. Now, fifty years later, he's a cultural lake, an impoundment of ideas and images and stories, and all the graduate students at Mississippi and all over the world are out sport fishing on Lake Faulkner.

Soon we see the bridge in the distance, and we know the six-mile float is over. There's a local fishing next to where we take out, and Greg drops a paddle as he steps from his canoe. We watch it circulate in a strong eddy just out of reach. If it were warmer we'd just jump in and grab it, but we made it this far high and dry. Finally we borrow the guy's fishing net to pull the errant paddle back to shore.

As we ride back up to Sardis Dam, I register with my paddling buddies Dixon and Greg a little exhilaration brought on by our canoe trip, but I admit to them that I'm not feeling very Faulknarian about the Little Tallahatchie. I write personal essays and prefer non-fiction narratives about nature to fiction leaning heavily on setting or place, like *Go Down Moses* or *Deliverance*. I don't make up rivers. I paddle them. After I get off the living stream, I worry the recorded details of my river trips into stories. A river is an ancient thing, much more

15

ancient than the human impulse to craft experience into narratives. Some writers (and I've come to realize I'm one of them) are captive to what Harvard eco-critic Laurence Buell has called "the environmental imagination," an impulse to see an encompassing nature as the great background for the fairly short-lived history of human endeavor. Faulkner believed in his Noble Prize eternal verities, "the human heart in conflict with itself," the country of the human imagination, but I just can't trust it the way he did.

As I pack up to drive down to Jackson, I think how in an odd way I'm very "Faulknarian," still susceptible to eternal verities. I think that I really believe a good writer can redeem a diminished landscape through writing it, that as a nature writer I can visit a place like the Little Tallahatchie, and write it and return to those who read what's lost in this country on the fringe of the Delta. I can find, so to speak, the wildness in it and concentrate on that. But what really remains of a scrap of storied wilderness once the logging trains, the skidders move in on it? What's lost once the Corps of Engineers has dammed the river? My day on the river has shown me it's often more than we think.

Soon as I get in my rental car to rejoin my book tour and my small-scale literary life the redemption I've gained diminishes with every mile I drive away from the river. Out to the interstate, I try to hold it by remembering how Dixon told me about the Little Tallahatchie, how it flattens out, slips down the Yazoo Bluffs, joins the Yazoo River, and then how the Yazoo slides out on the vast Delta flood plain, bends into deep meanders and slows down to a sluggish crawl south before disappearing ceaselessly into the Mississippi's deep dark flow.

But as we floated along, Dixon also reminded me that real rivers work hard for a living in Mississippi, absorbing fertilizer run-off, pesticides, anything that industrial agriculture that drains off crops and soil. "One big field curving into the body of the continent," that's how Dixon describes his home country, the lower Mississippi Delta.

Driving my rental car and touring around on the interstate I'm no redeemer. I'm only an active member of that continent's living body who cares for rivers, an interested visitor from far away. There's something in the force of that caring that makes even a brief float like this one part of something important. Waters still flow, even in the overworked, overburdened Delta.

Driving down to Jackson, my mind plays a trick on me. The asphalt is dark water and the eighteen-wheelers are industrial barges rolling past. My fantasy leaves me longing again for transformation, not simply redemption. I have to admit I want real rivers to run free. I want all the dams gone and all the fields free of the industrial chemicals that follow gravity into streams through run-off. Then the fantasy passes and I remember my day with Dixon and Greg on the Little Tallahatchie and something in that experience, that flash of memory, gives me the will to drive on.

THE WILD PIEDMONT

I've been reading Jack Turner's book of essays, *The Abstract Wild*. It's a collection of studied, passionate responses to the loss of the wild earth, from the high reaches of Tibet to his own backyard in Jackson, Wyoming. Turner, a climber and former philosophy professor, accepts that the worldwide destruction of wilderness and biodiversity has "spawned a powerful movement to protect what remains of wildness..." But for Turner, this movement does not go far enough. "We must do more," he argues. "We must examine processes at the heart of modernity that are only vaguely understood, however pernicious their consequences for the wild earth, processes that not only destroy the wild but diminish our experience of the wild."

With my particular interests (Southeastern piedmont rivers, land use issues, and environmental education to name a few), I tend to wander into such dense snarls of contrariness. I like to walk the edges of ideas about nature and culture, though I usually come back some place close to Aldo Leopold's famous land ethic when I circle home: "A thing is right when it tends to preserve the integrity, stability, and beauty of the biotic community. It is wrong when it tends otherwise."

Turner knows Leopold well. He's covered what he calls "the nature writer's canon," though you get the feeling that one reason the philosopher wrote *The Abstract Wild* is that Turner saw that no one had cut quite the same trail through the deep woods as he could. Thoreau, Edward Abbey, John Muir, and Wendell Berry all had angles on the problem, but they all stopped short of the solutions Jack Turner could articulate through his collective insight. Turner acknowledges all these masters—and many more. Most powerfully he explains how in his mid-forties, reading the essay on "deep, long range ecology" by philosopher Arne Naess, he was led to quit his university teaching job and try to find the wild by guiding climbing trips into the Tetons and other mountains all over the world. But in the end the ideas articulated in Naess's "Deep Ecology" are too tame for Jack Turner; the human world for him is compromised and ugly, and there is little of our culture that is not guilty of waging war against the wild.

In Turner's central essay—"The Abstract Wild: A Rant," he even implicates "us," those who believe in conservation and "smart growth" among the pernicious out to wage war against the wild. He suggests that there is no true wildness in what is now being called "nearby nature"—those "green spaces" where we build trails on flood plain acres and marginal woods incorporated centuries ago into development formulas yet still somehow bypassed by malls and subdivisions and interstate highways.

All the land we experience in urban and suburban "green" areas is still at some deep level controlled by market forces and subject to human mediation. Human legal documents set the rules for governing private land under conservation easements—so many structures, so much timbering, so many roads. The legislatures of modern states set the rules for national parks, and when we do visit our national parks all we experience is a "severely diminished wilderness... a caricature of its former self." National parks, wildlife preserves, sanctuaries, and refuges are, for Turner, really "mega-zoos" created for tourists and always under stress from human use, loved to death. I could find little room in Turner's reasoning to feel good about national parks, much less land trusts, green buildings and Earthfare grocery stores, because something "vast and old is vanishing" under our very watch.

Turner is not a total cynic. He's not willing to give the national parks over to the bulldozers, dissolve the easements, and abandon the sustainability movement. He's glad all that's around. It just doesn't go far enough. It answers the wrong questions, and worst of all, it's a poor substitute for the real thing. And what should our response be to the great loss of wild nature? "Our rage should mirror that loss," Turner says. Those who truly love the wild earth should get angry. "Anger nourishes hope and fuels rebellion," Turner says. "It presumes a judgment, presumes how things ought to be and aren't, presumes a caring."

As I write this I sit on the edge of a large Piedmont flood plain reflecting on Jack Turner's "wildness." It's still dark out there, and beyond my study windows I can't see far out into the flat expanse of open space below our house, but I know it's still covered with big timber and populated with deer, raccoons, possums, beaver, mink, and at least one bobcat. I know that six or eight times a year the Lawson's Fork pulses out of its banks and claims the bottom land as it has for millions of years. I can hear the river moving through the trees on these occasions from my study window. It's not wildland as Jack Turner describes it, but for me these 100-year flood plains are a "landscape of hope," to steal a phrase from Wallace Stegner. I don't believe we've got much chance of recovering the suburbs, of clearing away the blight of fifty years worth of sprawl, but if we can just set all these flood plains aside, and then maybe the wild that survives in them will saturate our souls once again.

I found out last week I don't have to go to Jackson, Wyoming, to discover people in the Southern piedmont who are reflective and often angry about the loss of the wild in our own backyards. I was invited to speak to a meeting of the Southern Appalachian Forest Coalition, an organization uniting two dozen or so environmental groups from Alabama to Virginia. Formed in 1994, SAFC sees our Southern Appalachian legacy at risk from "mismanagement, excessive road building, and irresponsible land development." Using support from their members SAFC has created a vision for protecting and restoring land, native species, and the ecological processes of natural lands using GIS mapping and scientific analysis. They call their vision "Return the Great Forest" and use a beautiful full color, spiral-bound brochure to articulate it.

"The Return of the Great Forest" is indeed a remarkable vision and document. Using maps, text, and photographs, SAFC promotes the return of values that would recover and protect a healthy sustainable forest which, in turn, could provide habitat and support ecological processes necessary for all native plant and animal species. This Great Forest, running from Virginia to Alabama with the Appalachian mountain chain as its core, would offer opportunities for humans to enjoy these natural areas, and its establishment and support would afford gradual transitions from urban to more natural areas. "Our bequest to future generations," the SAFC writes in their brochure, "can and must be a vigorous and well-conceived effort to provide a landscape of sustainable forests that are healthy, diverse, and resilient."

I've been involved in conservation efforts for ten years in the upstate of South Carolina, but I somehow missed this bold vision of forest restoration so close to home. I've been on boards of two land trusts, and on my tenure with each there has been little talk of large, region-wide planning, little discussion of regional ecosystems or biodiversity, no talk whatsoever of restoring anything ancient and wild. There have been small successes—road plans shifted to avoid surviving isolated wetlands, parcels of land restricted by easement assuring survival of key historical and cultural and biological resources, boardwalks built through beaver ponds, Wal-Mart parking lots landscaped because of large-tract development ordinances. The organizations I've supported and helped shape policy for have focused locally and worked one small task at a time to "save" the upstate of South Carolina.

Most of my fellow board members are working citizens in urban piedmont South Carolina communities. Occasionally a scientist will be appointed to a board, but mostly around here those who set the direction of land use policy and practice are government employees, business people, or educators. These men and women care about the changing land uses and the loss of "special places" but often have little knowledge of the natural history and culture of this region, much less the complexities of Deep Ecology, old growth, or Turner's loss of wilderness.

Many of the supporters of upstate conservation organizations are skeptical of philosophers talking about wildness and coalitions cooking up bold environmental visions. Many who would write a letter to the editor in support of more money for parks would consider regional ideas about wildlife corridors and core wildernesses "fringe" to the efforts of the conservation groups that they are willing to support with donations. Maybe that's why groups like SAFC have had so little luck so far spreading the vision of the Great Forest into the upstate of South Carolina. There's little overlap of constituency. "My own perspective on wild nature derives from my experience there and time well spent with hunters, fishermen, naturalists, explorers, mountaineers, rangers, men and women from a variety of other cultures, artists, and wild animals," Jack Turner writes in the introduction to his book. Turner's choices for friends and neighbors sound like a crowd most would not recognize in the "core" suburbs of the upper piedmont.

The Southern Appalachian Forest Coalition and its local host organization, South Carolina Forest Watch, scheduled their meeting for a February Saturday in the community room at Earthfare on Pelham Road in Greenville, right smack dab in the middle of the Charlotte-to-Atlanta I-85 corridor, the mother of all sprawls. I had been asked to be their keynote speaker and so I'd driven over from Spartanburg. I was excited. Our community's "demographics" won't support an Earthfare grocery, so my thirty-minute drive would serve double duty— a sustainability field trip and speaking engagement. "Bring back something we can't get here," my wife Betsy had requested when I left the house.

When I pulled into the Earthfare parking lot I couldn't decide whether the grocery chain of gourmet food, organic produce, and imported cheeses is an outpost of progress or an "outer station" on Capitalism's new frontier, like Kurtz's collection camp for ivory in Conrad's *Heart of Darkness*. When I parked my truck did I become a bold warrior in the sustainability crusade or simply complicit in a kinder, gentler destruction of the earth? One thing was certain: when I opened my truck door I could hear the growth beast growling in every direction on Pelham Road—fast-food restaurants, the interstate, new subdivisions. The Great Forest was nowhere to be seen.

The interior of Earthfare is comforting though—the smell of organic coffee and fresh-baked bread, soft music, muted earth tones. Walking in, it's possible for a moment to forget about industrial food production and the wide aisles and big box fluorescent lights of the Super Wal-Mart right down the road. Don't get me wrong. I'm a supporter of the concept of Earthfare, though reading someone like Jack Turner makes me wonder if Earthfare, by locating in a strip mall on Pelham Road, really does much to support that part of me that longs for the wild. In the realm of grocery stores does an Earthfare fall short in the same ways a national park falls short? Is it merely, when all is said and done, a poor substitute for local markets like our great-grandparents would have known? That's a lot to think about between parking lot and community meeting room, but I had no choice. Jack Turner had set the juices flowing, and I was going to see this one through to the end.

The group was small, maybe twenty people, mostly young, half male, half female. Almost half those present were employed by member organizations of SAFC. They'd brought plenty of literature and posted maps on all the walls. Like me, they were all dressed for a hike—fleeces in various earth tones. When all the introductions were finished the SAFC program began with an inspiring DVD presentation of music and images by South Carolina Forest Watch member Butch Clay taken off-trail in an "inventoried roadless area" called Rock Gorge in the Chattooga River watershed. Its official designation means that Rock Gorge is eligible for study as wilderness designation, though what Butch calls "the power politics of some local groups" has kept it out of wilderness.

Butch has driven down from Chattooga country, the closest US Forest Service designated wilderness to the Earthfare. The place he'd photographed is wild—a short, deep gorge on the river's upper reaches reachable only by bushwhacking upstream—and I've always held some embarrassment when I run into Butch that I didn't penetrate this wildness once in the three years I was researching my book *Chattooga: Descending into the Myth of Deliverance River*. "The Wilderness Upstream," I called one of my chapters, but I stopped short of exploring Rock Gorge's secrets and instead settled for a hike on an easy trail across the Ellicott Rock Wilderness boundary. After seeing Ellicott's nineteenth-century "boundary stone," defining the corner of North Carolina, South Carolina, and Georgia, I turned around and retreated to my truck three miles downstream at the Burrell's Ford Campground parking lot so I could get back to "town" by the end of my day of research in the woods.

While Butch was showing his DVD, I glanced around the meeting room at the large GIS-generated maps of the Southern Appalachian Region—important biological sites, critical watersheds, significant reserves of old growth and potential old growth, currently protected lands, conservation areas. What struck me when I looked at the maps was that my place in Spartanburg was clearly within the gray mass that SAFC considers the "Southern Appalachian Region" study area. Yet on map after map, there was nothing significant in the extension of blue forming our outlying region—no old growth, no potential old growth, no important biological sites, no critical watersheds, no significant regional reserves of relatively intact or recoverable landscape conservation areas. We'd been written off—a territory clearly belonging to the vision but ceded to the enemy. It was hard for me to stay focused on Butch's images of Rock Gorge—one of those "important biological sites"—a full 100 miles from where I'd committed to circling my wagons. I felt like the lost patrol, cut off from any supplies, without any hope of survival.

What I talked about that day in Earthfare was my own new writing project—a book-length personal narrative called *Circling Home* which explores my own backyard—a suburban lot on a creek in Spartanburg, on the edge of a large privately owned flood plain. It's an accounting of our own attempt to live by as many sustainable codes as possible—green design, green house, green life, but it's also a chronicle of 10,000 years of human history in a circle with a two mile radius locating our house in the middle. It's not a narrative about the wild earth. There's nothing anyone could call wilderness within 100 miles of our house. Instead it's an attempt, as Robert Frost once asked, to decide "What to make of a diminished thing"—the Southern Piedmont, an area plowed, logged, paved, and leveled for 300 years.

Mine was a voice I'm not sure the SAFC members were used to hearing from the visionary territory of the Great Forest. As I talked about our place in a subdivision on an impaired piedmont creek we can't swim in, I described a narrative not of recovery or restoration but instead of attention and acceptance. I told them I thought on the outer edge of the Great Forest, what we call the piedmont, we should listen less to Edward Abbey for our inspiration and more to Henry David Thoreau— the later Thoreau of *Wild Fruits* in particular. I held up Jared

Diamond's *Collapse* and explained how the book gives us a 13,000-year perspective and how, even though the bulk of the narrative is about "collapsed" former societies—the Maya, The Anasazi, the Vikings in Greenland, the people on Easter Island—it is in the end essentially hopeful. Diamond believes we can learn to live with modernity—in spite of all the diminishments and devaluations and increasing ignorance Jack Turner cites in *The Abstract Wild*.

People enjoyed what I had to say. I think they liked the different perspective—with no mention from me of roadless areas, wilderness designations, or critical habitats. They filled out my little "circling home" survey asking them to consider the mile around their own houses—who owns the land, what was the last crop grown there, and when was that (for much of the piedmont was agricultural land fifty years ago), and is there any forest at all within their circle?

After I'd finished my presentation Butch Clay spoke first. He said that he wanted to compliment me on taking my stand in the piedmont but that he was still uncertain there was anything to praise or celebrate or study in this ragged, battered hulk of a landscape, and that he was glad he was headed back to the Chattooga in a few hours and leaving this doomed place behind. That's not exactly what he said, probably not even close, but that's the tone of it—to live in the piedmont is to live in a world too close to the edge of environmental ruin. As for Jared Diamond and his global environmental vision, Butch pointed out the door to Pelham Road and said if any of us just looked around we could see the collapse closing in right now.

What Butch said made me start thinking about my place in a different way. As I drove home on I-85, I felt as if the scales had been removed from my eyes and I saw interstate in a new way. What I saw out along I-85 wasn't integrated, stable, or beautiful. The ceaseless flow of traffic from Richmond to Birmingham slices across all the major river systems of the piedmont, creating a virtual "killing zone" for any wildlife moving downstream seasonally from mountains to midlands as they had done since the last ice age. I've always had dreams of black bears reestablishing populations along the Saluda, Enoree, Reedy, Tyger, and Pacolet Rivers. I know though that as long as I-85 flows north-south across these drainages the chances as slim. The wildlife populations below I-85 will always be cut off from their kin to the north—gray and red fox, bobcat, raccoon, deer, possum. I've seen them all dead in the south-bound lanes of I-85, trying to head east. Some make it, but most don't. If the Great Forest is going to be pushed east of I-85 it might have to mature without bears. It will remain diminished as it is now. If Aldo Leopold is correct with his land ethic, could all of the choices my neighbors have made in Spartanburg County for 300 years have been wrong?

After I turned off the interstate and headed south toward home, I began to feel a little better about my place. I left the interstate behind and negotiated a series of smaller and smaller roads until I dropped down to the creek and parked in our driveway, only thirty feet above the slow flow of the Lawson's Fork. I was home, and I'd bought back organic cheeses and local sausage and a "green" dish-washing liquid I'd never seen in any Spartanburg store. Betsy's request would be fulfilled.

Until that day at Earthfare, the voice emerging in *Circling Home* was one of conciliation and acceptance. I thought of the book, when finished, as a voice of settlement, but I understand how some at SAFC might have heard it as a voice of capitulation—caving in to the forces of reality that run parallel to their vision of the Return of the Great Forest. I'm not about to abandon that voice. I don't see my community that way. We in the piedmont are poised somewhere between wilderness and environmental blight. Our nature is diminished, but our Southern Piedmont culture has not collapsed. There is hope along this fringe of the Great Forest, and I plan to find it and report on it.

I now look to Jack Turner's *The Abstract Wild*, Butch Clay, and the members of SAFC for one important aspect of my vision of this region—but not for the entire vision. Their brochures have no pictures of the landscapes I find familiar and hopeful. Though they include my place in the Southern Appalachian Region, there are no pictures of smart-growth subdivisions, or second-growth woodlands that have somehow survived the saw, or piedmont creeks flowing boldly to the sea over bedrock shoals in spite of their waters stained red with the run-off from development upstream. I want the vision of the Great Forest to come to reconcile with us, just as I want the people intent on economic development and ignorant of the possibilities of the Great Forest to come to terms with it.

The Great Forest People have an anger fueled by wrongs begun hundreds of years in the past when land use habits were established in the piedmont and on the Blue Ridge mountain front. The SAFC is a group with a philosophy, like Jack Turner, who sees the efforts now underway by land trusts and smart growth organizations as falling far short of what is right and what needs to be done. Though they believe these organizations are sincere in our love for conservation, they also believe the issues we embrace are short-sighted—sprawl, smart growth, whatever you want to call it. The question of wildness is central to the earth for them. It is a radical question—if you take "radical" at its fundamental meaning—of the roots. These lovers of wildness and wild places are not kooks. They are not extremists. They have drawn a line around the Southern Appalachians and defined us—we are still, they claim, the Great Forest. Within the boundaries of who we are now is a surviving remnant wildness and the potential for a great deal more to be restored 500 years in the future—if only we can figure out where it might be. These are people with a deep vision to show us the way, and we need to listen to them if we are going to find a way to survive the next 13,000 years.

But I am not only one of the Great Forest People. I am from the Big Suburb, one day stretching from Washington, DC, to Atlanta. In that Big Suburb are the Big Box People, the Children of the Super Slab, the Fast Food Tribe, the Ornamental Conifer Purchased at the Wal-Mart People. There is a vision at work here as well—though it may not be as bold or striking. The millions of people, like me and my neighbors, on the fringes of the Southern Appalachian Region are not going to vanish, and most of us are not going to shop at Earthfare or join Upstate Forever, much less one of the organizations in SAFC. If the Great Forest is going to work for us, it better have a boat launch and deer stands and good roads. Like it or not, these two visions have to somehow be integrated for us all—animals, plants, and people—to survive.

The West, Wallace Stegner once said, is the landscape of hope. I hope he was wrong. I hope it's the South as well. I'd like to see hope someday walking down the watershed of the Lawson's Fork in the form of an adult black bear, headed right back up toward the heart of the Great Forest. And I'd like to think that the people of the edge of that creek—in suburbs like mine—will be glad to have him there, living in the bottom lands, passing through.

LAKE CONESTEE

Dave Hargett's dream for Lake Conestee isn't really visible from the parking lot of the Racecar Speedy Mart. The impressive nineteenth-century stone dam on the Reedy River in Greenville, South Carolina, is in clear view though, and the boarded-up textile mill, closed twenty years ago, crowds in everyone's line of site just off Conestee Mill Road. To anyone driving past, the eighteen of us—two Wofford College professors, fifteen college students, and Dave—look a little suspicious, standing among the fire ant mounds and stunted pines on the ridge above the river.

It's early fall and in only the minute or two we've stood with our fifteen freshmen looking out over the Reedy River we all consider beautiful, a great blue heron and red-tailed hawk have crossed paths low above what's left of the lake behind the dam. Appreciation of beauty in the natural world is something easy to teach. Convincing these students that they are somehow responsible for understanding and even correcting the sort of environmental disaster that is contained in the story of Conestee is more difficult and will take far longer.

Dave Hargett is up for it though. He's sent us links to the Conestee web site, and with my colleague Ellen Goldey's expertise as a toxicologist we've sorted through pages of environmental history. Slender and dressed comfortably for the field in chinos and hiking boots, Dave could just as easily be leading a bird walk as briefing a class on Conestee. He waves his arms and begins to tell us of the vision that has possessed a handful of people who have seen the potential here: a long corridor of greenway stretching for twenty-five miles from Furman University all the way to this depressed site.

We've prepped our students for the Conestee field trip, told them that environmental visions in South Carolina have been few and far between. It's a state known more for a Bible Belt faith in "economic development," no matter what the cost. A few families got rich off ventures like Conestee Mill, but the working people in the Upstate have suffered mightily through 200 years of industrial revolution—first the iron industry, then textiles, and now real-estate speculation. Unlike the ruling class, the poor have little to show for their role in what former Supreme Court Chief Justice Brennan once called "the war against the world." Wages have remained low and the old industrial communities—once thriving, though poor communities—turned blighted when industries left, chasing even cheaper wages overseas.

The waterways of upstate South Carolina have shown the strain of "progress" maybe most of all. Nearly all the rivers and creeks in the region are classified as impaired by the South Carolina Department of Health and Environmental Control (DHEC). All are unsafe to drink, and most aren't fit for swimming. Some still can't support aquatic life, thirty years after the Clean Water Act was meant to put a stop to wholesale exploitation of these waterways for greed and profit.

The discussion and this field trip are part of two required general education courses, biology and humanities, linked around a theme, in this case, "The Nature and Culture of Water." Ellen, in a former life, worked as a researcher for the Environmental Protection Agency, so she has a keen interest in toxins and has taught the students enough chemistry and fresh water ecology concerning the site to allow them to grasp its complexity as an industrial brownfield. Holding down the role of humanities professor, I've spent my class time talking about upstate environmental history, about issues of environmental justice and the complex set of values that allow a community to dam a river and then, in a little over a 100 years, destroy the lake behind the dam.

Two of the students, Thomas Pierce and Amelia Snyder, took the linked classes as freshmen, and now they're back as rising sophomores to assist. They help the other students grasp the material, give the linked courses some continuity through their two-year participation, and shoulder the weighty titles of "preceptors" for the courses. Today, their main role will be as kayak wranglers as we take the students out on the lake.

Dave, a local environmental engineer and activist, drives us behind the Speedy Mart and through a chain-link fence to a launch site on the impoundment's east lobe. We unload our boats and Dave gathers us at the water's edge and fills us in on the research to make the place real. He knows the history of this watery landscape, how in the 1940s, Lake Conestee (Cherokee for "beautiful water") was hundreds of acres of open water, a power source for the mill since the 1830s. It was also a recreational centerpiece for the community and a source of supplementary protein for the workers—fish and turtles.

Now, aerial photos show a fifty-year-old river-bottom forest maturing over thick sediment laid down by the Reedy over Greenville's busiest industrial decades. There's clay here from the clearing of the land for early agriculture, eroded off the Donaldson air base in the 1940s, the I-85 construction project of the late 1950s, and the industrial boom of the 1960s, all before there was any sediment control. And not only sediment came down the Reedy River channel to this first major dam below Greenville proper: there are also all the compounds used to create our current standard of living— lead, zinc, copper, and other heavy metals, PCBs and pesticides in vast quantities, all "stored" here behind the thick Conestee mill dam.

The students take notes as Dave tells us about the vision for "Conestee Park" as we look back upstream toward the horizon line marking the spot where water courses down the old dam's face. What Dave sees when he looks toward the dam is the silted-in lake above, a place with boatable water and wildlife habitat. Working with the Conestee Foundation, the nonprofit that has purchased the lake, Dave envisions hiking and biking trails and an ecological education center on the 300 acres of slough, island, shoreline, and mud flat near what he says will be the urban center of the city of Greenville in 2020.

We fit everybody into their kayaks. Thomas and Amelia go through a safety talk and check to make sure all the PFDs (personal flotation devices) are snug and secure. These are stable lake kayaks, so we don't see any trouble with navigating the calm lake and river. Howard, a large basketball player, can't get his feet in his boat, so we switch him into a longer one. Amelia makes a joke about how if Howard's boat somehow sinks he can paddle one of his sneakers back to shore.

As we launch our boats, I sort the complex smells of this place: peat or sewage? Somewhere below in the sediment is what Dave calls "black mayonnaise," a layer of sludge laid down since 1892, years before Greenville treated the discharge from its sewage plant positioned a few miles upstream. This sewage savannah, this delta of deadly compounds, holds all the sins of the industrial upstate, washed downstream and deposited like sand where the current slowed behind the Conestee dam. As we paddle upstream I learn, once again, that we're all downstream from something, somebody.

On the water it's like paddling in Africa, not upstate South Carolina. The Conestee sloughs open up into bays fringed by yellow periwinkle and a backdrop of mature oaks and poplars. Dave points out that the periwinkle, though beautiful, is not native. It's an intrusive weed species. Ellen agrees, but notes that it's hiding all the Conestee trash—cans, Styrofoam, bottles, balls of every sort: football, golf, soccer, basketball, anything that will float.

We cruise around the bay, and I'm baffled by how much something can change in my mind from ugly to beautiful by just cruising into the middle of it. From shore, this old silted-in industrial reservoir looks like a wasteland, not a wonderland, or "oasis," as Dave keeps calling it. Then there is a whistle of a red-tailed hawk as we cruise close to where a nest is hidden. The bird's call brings me back to Dave's dreams. I hear something and turn—a turtle big as an old black skillet lumbers down off the bank into the water.

After the hawks have fallen silent, we portage over a narrow strand of hardwoods like early explorers, dragging our boats from the bay to an old river channel and paddle upstream. Birds are everywhere and they seem not to mind the sewage sludge below, though tissue samples from fish this summer will show more of what we can't see. Ellen circles everyone together and reminds them that what we're hiking over is what the toxicologists call "bio-magnification," concentrations of contaminants, all the way up the food chain, a little Rachael Carson nightmare, right here in our own backyard. The bird life is abundant: little green herons, great blue herons, cormorants, all eating fish. Dozens of "woodies," the wood ducks whose boxes rise upward every few hundred yards of shoreline, cruising these waters and grazing the duckweed. Along the shore are the ones we can't see: tracks of deer, raccoon. Dave tells me stories of seeing otters swimming in these very waters.

We land the boats, gather the group, bushwhack a few yards and hit a well-traveled four-wheeler trail circling an island in the old lake's north corner. There are red flags through the woods, signs of an archeological survey showing that Archaic and Woodlands people lived here, working quartz and imported chert, making pottery, hauling in soapstone from quarries in the upstate. This high spot on the island is where Dave hopes to put some sort of structure for environmental education, high above the wetlands and the river. I look around and note the loveliness of these neglected woods. Full summer's green expanse closes in around us.

Back on the river Thomas, leading the way in his kayak, follows a pair of wood ducks. Some of us get close enough to see the way they drag one wing in the water, faking injury to draw us away from their young ones, hiding in the mats of flowers. These cycles go on—birth, the raising of the young. And what of our young? Why have so few seen wood ducks perform to protect the summer's brood? "One hundred thousand school children are within a thirty-minute bus ride of this place," Dave says.

I look back at our line of kayaks strung out along the Reedy River. We are like a flock of brightly colored water birds following Dave in his green canoe. Headed back to the launch site, we slosh through the flowers and mud to cut through to the bay where we started. We slide our boats behind us, and several of us sink down in the sludge, knee-deep. The week before we'd introduced the class to the Earth Charter, an idea that originated in 1987, then shown several dozen cascading pledges packed into a teal and white tri-fold brochure. We told them this charter was the result of years of negotiation among a wide variety of people and organizations and nations to articulate the complexity of a world environmental vision. "We stand at a critical moment in Earth's history," the Earth Charter states in the preamble, "a time when humanity must choose its future."

The summer before Ellen and I had been two of a group of academics one hundred strong in Chewonki, Maine. We were professors, administrators, college presidents, gathered to talk about the Earth Charter. Our goal was what conference organizer Peter Corcoran called "the urgency of moving higher education toward sustainability." On the first night Thomas Berry and Stephen Rockefeller were keynote speakers. Rockefeller spoke first as introduction. As one of the key architects of the Earth Charter, in his remarks he described the charter as "the most negotiated document in human history."

35

Ecotheologian Thomas Berry stood up to speak next. He was an old soul, hunched, closing in on ninety years of age. In his clear voice he brought his idea of "the Great Work" into the room. It's been his life work, a search for a planetary ethic. Above us that night hung the imposing skeleton of a fin whale killed by a freighter off Virginia. "When we are all gone, the memory I will have is of the whale," Berry said, "the guardian spirit and presence." He described creation as "a communion of subjects rather than a collection of objects," a perspective necessary for the "long-term flourishing of the earth's human and ecological communities."

Later in the week, professor of religion and ecology Mary Evelyn Tucker called the Earth Charter "a song of hope" and stated that "we need to hear, play and dance to that music." She explained how the Earth Charter could be used possibly as "soft law," like an "international declaration of planetary rights." Or it could be used as an educational tool if a conference like the one at Chewonki was successful. As she explained it, the Earth Charter pulled together many concerns and common hopes.

From that Maine conference, we brought back our own song of hope—that our students would hear the importance of not only thinking critically about environmental issues. We wanted them to feel deeply as well. We wanted them to fall in love with our abused, neglected Piedmont landscape. So with our students we discussed how difficult it is to find common ground among all the world's citizens, and now at Conestee I think of Thomas Berry and his book *The Dream of the Earth*: "We are returning to our native place after a long absence, meeting once again with our kin in the earth community." I remind myself that the promise of the Earth Charter and Thomas Berry's earth community includes these wood ducks and the hawks as great citizens of this watery commonwealth. These dreams even include the bacteria working in the sludge below the lake's neglected surface.

As we land our boats, I hear the water over the Conestee dam just downstream, see the top of the old abandoned cotton mill. There is so much beauty here, but also so much uncertainty about what is under the surface. That's the ugliness—what we don't know, what we can't afford to clean up. I take one last look at Lake Conestee before loading the boats. It's as if the whole long history of our exploitation of the Piedmont is contained here in these images, these sounds. It will take decades of deep earth dreams to restore Conestee to a vision of wholeness, but those who have learned to love the lake seem up to it. We'll return here each year and float these sloughs and listen for the red-tail's whistle.

A HOLE IN TIME

"I'm pretty confident I'm in the Pleistocene," Terry Ferguson says when I ask how deep in time he's standing. Terry is in an excavated pit. The dirt walls are straight, angular, and stair-step steeply downward toward the past like a drawing for a book explaining Euclidian geometry. The Pleistocene, the geologic epoch Terry invokes, ended about thirteen thousand years ago when glaciers covered about 30 percent of the earth and the climate here in Pickens County, South Carolina, was as cool as Minnesota. Terry says the visual scale of time he's etched on the dirt walls of this hole shows how "about every ten inches we go down, we're back another thousand years."

When not deep in a vanished epoch, Terry works with me at Wofford College where he's had academic lives as a geologist, an archeologist/anthropologist, and an instructional technology expert. Now the two of us, both in our mid-fifties, have changed jobs. We anchor the new environmental studies major, an interdisciplinary program where people like us from different disciplines explore environmental problems together.

This "dig" is some of Terry's ongoing professional research and there are plenty of environmental questions to work on here—how exactly did people from different ages live in this place, being one of the big ones. We're hoping we can find several ways that this place and Terry's on-going work here can fit easily into our new environmental studies program.

There are six of us on-site today, myself included. I'm observing, asking questions, sitting up in the Holocene, the present epoch, on a shovel-carved lip of dark Southern piedmont alluvial soil just above the Oolenoy River. My feet rest ten or twelve inches deeper on tawny sediments. It's about twelve hundred years to the bottoms of my boots, according to Terry's time scale.

Though fixed solidly in time, I feel a little out of place. Everyone but me is a regular, here to work. This morning Terry shares this pit with Tommy Charles and Wesley Burnett. Tommy's soon to be retired from the South Carolina Institute of Archaeology and Anthropology in Columbia, and this is one of the many projects he is still tending. Tommy and Terry are the professional archeologists on this project—officially known as 38PN35, scientific shorthand for the thirty-fifth site investigated in Pickens County—and they've been digging together here for four years. Wes is a retired Clemson geography professor and seasoned archaeological volunteer. When he's not down in the hole, he's sitting on top of an overturned bucket reading a long history of the Middle East, one of his geographical research interests.

Below the seat of my jeans, in a space about the thickness of the book Wes has been reading, all our American/European history disappears downward—the Iraq War (the present–2004), the Summer of Love (1968), World War II (1945–1941), the Civil War (1865–1861, what some unreconstructed locals still call "the late unpleasantness"), the American Revolution (1781–1776), the founding of Charleston (1670), Desoto's journey inland to the Mississippi River (1540). Below that, it's Native American occupation—Cherokee, Mississippian, Woodland, Archaic, Paleo—ten feet down to Terry's clammy Pleistocene floor.

Terry loves research, and he discovered early on that he was good at it. He arrived at Wofford in 1971 thinking he wanted to major in psychology, but he quickly found out that the behaviorists were in power. "I wanted Jung and depth psychology, and I wasn't very interested in running rats," he's said. He tried physics, but after working on Broad River rock shelters during a January term sponsored by Wofford's legendary geologist John Harrington, he became interested in archaeology and geology. The summer before his junior year he worked at an archeological field school in New Mexico and used his nine hours credit to anchor a major in sociology. Even after he chose sociology, Terry's intellectual interests stayed broad, including upper-level English classes in which he studied James Joyce. "I've always been interested in the mind of man," Terry says, "but I ended up looking at the mind of the earth."

For his masters work at the University of Tennessee, Terry wrote about soapstone quarries in northwestern South Carolina. His dissertation at Tennessee is on prehistoric settlement patterns on the Cumberland Plateau of Tennessee and Kentucky. Back at Wofford in the mid-eighties, Terry continued John Harrington's tradition of teaching geology as a liberal arts science, though he never lost his love of "depth" in any intellectual form.

More important than our professional affiliation, Terry and I are good friends and this trip to the Pleistocene is another scene in an on-going conversation that goes back over twenty years. I know just enough about science to keep Terry interested, and he's read most of the authors I admire, particularly the early modernists. Maturing in the age of Freud, the modernists pioneered the idea of depth in literature through the metaphor of conscious/unconscious. "I should have been a ragged claw scuttling across the floors of silent seas," T. S. Eliot wrote in "The Love Song of J. Alfred Prufrock." Terry's no ragged claw deep in his hole, but the idea of going down in order to get enlightenment or knowledge is something that engages him as well as me.

Our conversations often wander backward (or downward) in time—to past cultures, past extinctions, past problems. Terry knows that the human mind, and the culture it's created, has always served as its own pit worthy of excavation. I'm no scientist and he's no poet/literary intellectual, but in our shared worlds we often find a place to stand together.

This excavated hole in time is such a place. It charges Terry up intellectually and it gives me a place from which I can dream all the way down to a vanished epoch. "You can't get there from here," is the old adage for those lost in a foreign place. The pit is some place I can go and leave the present behind. Down where Terry stands there were families, alliances, and conversations 10,000 years before now. We'll never know exactly what they said, but I can come close to the spirit of it all by listening to what's been discovered here. "It's a layer cake," Terry says. "Shadows upon shadows. Each inch contains four generations. Same spot, but different people."

Terry works to find the metaphor to explain it all. "I see dead people," I want to interject humorously into Terry's discussion about the Early Archaic period, but I know I shouldn't.

Time's arrow, Stephen Jay Gould calls the horizontal way mortals often view our passing lives. In this metaphor the present is the head of an arrow shooting through space into the future, pulling the lengthening shaft of the past behind it. Yet it seems when time is viewed on a mythic or religious scale it's almost never horizontal, with heaven above and hell usually below. Here in Pickens County, Terry's metaphor for time is mythic, a deep, stair-stepping hole in the earth, the bottom of which is about the size of a phone booth floor.

The site of Terry's hole, the Robertson Horse Farm, is truly a pastoral spot in this upcountry South Carolina world turning quickly suburban. The farm's sits in a broad valley up against the Blue Ridge mountain front where the Oolenoy and South Saluda Rivers come together. The long farm road into the site runs through fertile bottomland fields, and the flatness of the flood plain carries your eye not down but out until it stalls against a sharp line of blue sky and the green ridges confining the rivers.

As Terry narrates from below, I watch Wesley use a large kitchen spoon to remove a "feature" about two feet above where Terry stands. Wesley puts spoon after spoon of dark alluvial dirt in a large white cloth bag for later analysis off-site. Above their heads, in the present, horses graze in adjacent pastures. They're kept out of the archeological site by electric fences. A chestnut stallion keeps vigil at the back fence where volunteer Roger Lindsay mans the screens. He examines every bucket of dirt they pull out of the hole for small flakes of worked stone.

Roger's a retired paint contractor who now lives nearby, and he has been with the dig from the beginning. His interest in prehistory is quite practical—as an avocation he's a "flintknapper" who makes projectile points and replica stone tools for his own pleasure and understanding. He's so good at primitive technology that his replicas are in museums, and he's won contests for throwing accuracy using an atlatal, the ancient "throwing stick" used for hunting and warring, the forerunner of the bow and arrow by tens of thousands of years. In his pickup, Roger always keeps a full array of bows, arrows, and atlatals made from the similar local materials that the originals would have utilized. "He knows so much about the way they worked I think Roger's channeling these people," Terry explained to me once.

Jesse Robertson, who owns land across the river, sits in an old deck chair and observes the scene as I do. Jesse is another loyal volunteer who has also worked this site since 2004. Jesse contributes much more than his volunteer labor to this project. He has arranged a metal carport over the site to give it shade and protect it from the rain, and it makes a nice place to take a break or observe.

A few years earlier Jesse had been clearing this bottom for his brother while Terry and Tommy were working the land on the South Saluda River just downstream from its confluence with the Oolenoy. He'd yanked up a tree trunk and tangled in its roots was a shard of fiber-tempered pottery. He collected it, and told Terry exactly where it was found. Fiber tempered pottery had never been reported in this far from the Savannah River, so the team secured permission to move the excavation to this terrace above the Oolenoy. The site has proven rich in artifacts and information with evidence of settlement from historic time all the way back ten thousand years.

Just to Jesse's right is a line of holes where a Woodland Period palisade, or log fort, surrounded a village here about seven hundred years ago. Seven holes are exposed and survey flags mark the location of several others behind us. We sit and watch from just outside the walls of that old Indian log fort. Seven hundred years is a long time, but it's not much on a deep time scale. Figuring twenty years a generation, the people who felt secure behind this stockade were separated from the people at the bottom of Terry's pit by the passing of around 550 lifetimes.

Everyone's excited today because thirty inches higher than the floor Tommy and Terry stand on is a perfectly excavated tabletop of silt and sand around a formation of sixteen stones placed there by deliberate human hands ten thousand years in the past. The stones look a little like a patio, though no larger than a living room end table. Chris Clement, a colleague of Terry and Tommy's, had been working this site on contract when the feature was discovered two years ago. Jesse says that the stone feature was such an unexpected surprise that those working that day joked it had to be a landing pad for a prehistoric space ship. Tommy and Terry have been asking their colleagues in the Southeast what it could be, and nobody has a clue. Today, Terry and Tommy plan to remove it.

"It's something someone placed here," Terry says. They know the feature's date because the team has already removed half the stones and underneath they found charcoal from conifers and hardwoods, and a hickory nut fragment. Radiocarbon testing gave them the ten thousand BP (before present) date associated with the feature, the oldest culturally associated radiocarbon date in South Carolina. That places the stones near the beginning of what's known as the Archaic Period of human prehistory.

As Terry and Tommy's work on this site demonstrates, archaeology is a science balanced between theory and method—"find, excavate, analyze," as Terry explains it. As a science, it's very different from the image we get watching Indiana Jones movies. Literary romance is often hard to come by amidst the dust and sweat of work with shovels, trowels, and dental picks. They've been at it here for four years, and this hole in the ground, several tons of excavated soil, and a few hundred small plastic bags of artifacts and carbonized botanical samples are all they physically have to show for their labor.

When I ask about the slow pace and stop-and-start nature of this project, Terry points out that many in the archeological profession are in cultural resource management, hired-guns, masters-level researchers working on contracts to meet the needs of a government permit for construction projects. For the most part, CRM archaeology is good, but it's always done within the constraints of a particular project. Once the project is finished, the reports generated often end up as "gray literature," information not available to the public because the results belong to who paid for them or few find the funds or time to publish the results.

The kind of archaeology Terry's been conducting in Pickens County is another side of the profession, what he calls "purposeful research," and it has none of the constraints of CRM work. "You pick a particular site that will answer particular questions," he explained to me as we drove over to

Pickens this morning, "and you work it repeatedly when there is time and money."

"Is a feature an artifact?" a large man with a Santa Claus beard asks. He's standing opposite from me above the pit. He's shown up this morning to see what the scientists are doing down in this Pickens County pit. He's been introduced as a serious artifact hunter, and he's curious as to what they've turned up so deep in the earth. 38PN35 has been known since the late 1800s as a location rich in artifacts, and people have been "surface collecting" the fields and pastures for over a hundred years. What they all found "arrowhead hunting" is mostly lost to the professional archaeology community, scattered among a thousand private collections.

"No, a feature's a feature," Terry clarifies. "It's something we find that's human-made. It could be the site of a fire, a cache of decayed plant matter, a posthole, or something else. Somebody dug a pit here where the soil's dark. And somebody laid these stones on top of it. Actually, a feature can tell us a great deal more than projectile point can."

I can see this man's mind processing what Terry has said. He spends his time looking for artifacts on the surface of bottomland fields like this one. He collects projectile points—what everyone used to call arrowheads—also potsherds, ground stones, objects. The work here, the systematic archaeological exploration of a site, is something he hasn't thought about much. The past for him is the left over (and often valuable for trade or commerce) detritus of occupation, like a landlord cleaning out a rental house and selling what's left behind at the flea market.

What Terry's interested in is the layers of the occupation. "It's not the artifacts," Terry's said. "It's where the artifacts are." Terry knows that there is so much information available to a careful researcher, things that an artifact hunter could never know about a long-vanished cultural moment, in this case the beginning of the Holocene, ten thousand year before the present.

"I can't imagine ten thousand years into the future," Tommy Charles adds, musing suddenly about time in the other direction. He's shoulder-to-shoulder with Terry looking up out of the 10-foot-deep excavation pit. "I know there will be blue sky, clouds. What else? That's about as far as I can get."

I write down Tommy's words in my notebook and think for a moment about my own sense of time. I'm in the humanities, a creative writer, but I've been on enough archaeology sites like this one and taken enough geology classes to have what some would consider a well-developed sense of the past—what I like to call "deep time." I'm never at a loss when thinking back ten thousand years, and I especially like time when it's layered in depositional sediment like it is on the Oolenoy River, an inch for every hundred years.

I'm fifty-three and my half-inch of time/sediment shows up quite well here at the surface of this site, though it looks precarious on the lip of the dig, as if my life could blow away or be scooped up in seconds.

But the future? I can't get much further than Tommy. My sense of future time plays out too often in Jetsons fantasies of flying cars and personal convenience, but most times I have no idea where the arrowhead is flying. "The future," as I heard one prognosticator say recently, "is always someone's fiction."

What does the story of the next one hundred, much less ten thousand years, hold for valleys such as this one in the fast-growing piedmont of South Carolina? My interest in the future usually focuses on land use and environment and population, and here in the valley of the Oolenoy the stories the prognosticators are floating are not all happy—more people and pollution to come. Less biodiversity. Global warming.

So what can the past tell us about the future? The band of Archiac nomads who laid these stones probably included at most thirty or forty individuals. There may have been more than one band in a watershed, or maybe there was only one. We know that they moved seasonally up and down river systems searching out available food. They may have crossed into other watersheds for resources, such as stone for making tools. They hunted and gathered shellfish, berries, roots, and such. Their way of life was appropriate for the area's resources and probably persisted for many thousands of years with little change. For modern Holocene humans like us, our lives are changing daily, and our supply lines grow thinner every day.

I look down from above and try to find my own pattern in the intentional arrangement of the Archaic stones. I grasp for some hint into the Stone Age mind that placed this pavement here. These people who lived ten thousand years ago had the same mental capacities as I have. They weren't "primitive" in the way we've always meant that word— backward, underdeveloped, simple. Their evolved culture had pushed their technology and hunting/gathering as far as resources allowed. It's sites like this rich in information that can slowly help fill in some of the blank spaces.

I like to imagine that this arrangement of stones was recreational—almost like the Stone Age patio it resembles—or a ceremonial or religious spot. It could be a sweat lodge or altar or an old-time geocache. I can sense how pleasant it would have been to sit on what Terry's excavation has discovered was a small bluff above the river ten thousand years ago.

Terry makes sure I understand that poetic revelries are fine, but they don't know what's below the stones. He can see that something was buried there because the excavation has already taken off the side of the feature, exposing the faint outline of a pit filled with discolored soil. "It could be a cremation or a bundle of artifacts. It could be something else," Terry says. He says they may find out what it is when they remove the remaining stones, or the answer could be found when they excavate down to the bottom level of the small pit, or they may get some clarity when the data comes back from botanical analysis months later—or, as Terry admits, "We may never really know."

Later in the day as Terry removes the first of the sixteen stones, I remember when I sat at Crazy Creek in the Cirque of the Towers high in Wyoming's Wind River Range many years ago and watched as my archeologist friend and his brother John ascended a two thousand foot rock pinnacle, a remnant of the Ice Age, carved by Pleistocene glaciers. It took them all day as I watched through binoculars. What was it? Sixteen years ago? It was a long time for time's arrow to fly on anybody's personal time scale.

All day Terry, the geoarcheologist, and his brother, the geophysist, climbed hard rock higher and higher through the clear Wyoming summer air, and the poet took notes below. The irony of it all was that when they arrived on the top of their spire, they were standing, as Terry was now, on the Pleistocene.

As I reassemble that long-ago trip I remember how we fished most days for trout in high alpine lakes, and what we caught we kept fresh in a snow bank left over from the winter before at eleven thousand feet. Up there in the high Cirque we were hunter/gatherers for two weeks. We caught our own meat, camped in temporary shelters, talked around campfires. Instead of furs, we wore expensive petroleum-based designer fleeces to keep warm. Instead of discussing kinship, we talked of books we'd read and past trips into the wilderness.

In reality, it was hard to leave the Holocene behind. No matter how much we wanted to be romantics about our time in the Wyoming wilderness, we knew there were two or three dozen other climbers who possessed permits and had also hiked ten miles into the Cirque over two twelve thousand foot passes to camp and scale the famous wild peaks.

This federally designated wilderness was under the same types of population pressures that Pickens County will suffer in the future. A ranger told us not to drink unfiltered water from the wilderness lake at the center of the Cirque because the bacteria levels—particularly fecal coliform—were disturbingly high that summer from all the human activity of the climbers.

As I sit by this hole in time, I feel like I know these Archaic campers, and I think of them as a band of Stone Age brothers and sisters. I know this is dangerous, that now is now, and then was then, but I can't help it. It's my natural inclination. It's the mark of my tribe—to imagine, to teleport back and forward to all ages, to see through time.

Back in the present Terry and Tommy remove the pavement of stones from the feature. They bag and number each stone in its own freezer bag, then label with site number, location, and date. As Terry picks them up they often crumble in his hands. He puts all the pieces in the bags. They take dozens of pictures. Each time they take a picture they place the little striped black and white plastic arrow for scale, always pointing north, and write the relevant scene description on the small white marker board they call a mug board.

The most exciting moment for me comes when Terry pries up one stone with his trowel and it's clear that it's been split perfectly in half to make it level with the others. One edge has also been chipped away so it would fit perfectly with the stones next to it. Someone did this ten thousand years ago. Someone cared that the pavement of stones was level.

"Was the leveling aesthetic or practical?" My question doesn't seem to interest Terry much, and he continues to remove all the remaining stones.

After two hours, 35PN38's mysterious early Archaic feature—carefully exposed for the first time in ten thousand years—finally disappears into two peach crates. "Archaeology's actually a little sad," Terry says as he places the last stone and climbs out of the pit. "It destroys the past in order to understand it."

We pack all the equipment in two wheelbarrows and push them across the horse pasture to our vehicles. One more day and this crew of scientists and volunteers will shut the site down since they're down to the end of their current funding.

In order to limit their impact on Jesse's land, Terry's research team has brought in a Porta-John, and it sits just outside the last fence next to the parking area. Tommy goes to take a leak before he hits the road back to Columbia.

Our arrowhead-hunting Santa Clause chats with Roger about the tools he's made. He walks to his truck and returns with three atlatals and some six-foot long "darts" that fit on the throwing sticks. The atlatals are about eighteen inches long, and he's fitted each with rawhide loops for two fingers. The throwing stick lengthens the arm, like those plastic tennis ball throwers dog owners use. As we look at Roger's handiwork, he hooks his fingers in the rawhide loops and points out with pride how one of the counter weights on this, his favorite atlatal, was shaped from soapstone to the same pattern as one found right here on the site.

"Turkey feathers," Santa Clause says, running his finger over the guide feathers on one of the darts.

"The shafts are made from river cane cut right in this valley," Roger says, placing the six-foot long dart on the throwing stick.

"Throw it," Santa Clause says, and points at a clay bank fifty yards away.

Roger hops a couple of times and lets fly. The dart sails, flutters a little, and sticks soundly in the clay bank. Roger smiles with pride, and all of us watching give a little tribal whoop.

As Roger retrieves his ancient dart from the clay bank, I look around the valley of the Oolenoy, and it's obvious why these ancient people shaking free of the Pleistocene camped here on their long migrations up from the Atlantic coast—the land is so rich in natural beauty. Surely resources such as beauty mattered to them.

No matter how many Holocene humans move into this watershed it will still be beautiful. There will always be this bright blue summer sky, and a tree line in the distance. That much we know. The rest of our lives will disappear into the ground or the atmosphere.

Even the pit Terry and Tommy have excavated won't last. Jesse has a backhoe ready to cover it up once the archeologists are done with it. But those post holes still visible from that seven-hundred-year-old stockade show me that if you want to leave a mark on the land, dig a hole, so I dig the toe of my boots into the ground at my feet. I've pushed down five hundred years or so before Terry bids his friends and colleagues goodbye for the day. I left no artifacts behind to mark my visit to the Oolenoy, and the feature I make with my boot won't last out the decade, much less Tommy's ten thousand years.

II

In my darkest night,
when the moon was covered
and I roamed through the wreckage,
a nimbus-clouded voice
directed me:
"Live in the layers,
not on the litter."

—Stanley Kunitz
From "The Layers"

COACHWHIP

Padgett Powell's need to be comfortable hits him just before we start walking the final half-mile to the abandoned rock quarry, so he changes clothes with the pickup's door open between his boxer shorts and Betsy, David's sister. The blue rain jacket borrowed from me is the first to go, draped over the open passenger door. It's finally stopped raining, and the May sun is out.

When Padgett emerges from behind the dark blue door, he is finally dressed for Southern summer in his long khaki shorts he has worn on the flight the day before. He has on a khaki shirt and a wide, brown leather belt cinched up a notch more than necessary. I look down and he is also wearing what he calls his "coachwhip catching shoes," a well-worn set of Docksiders with no socks.

Then Padgett takes off down the trail behind Ab, David, and Betsy. Padgett's mood seems reflective, even somber. Maybe he is expectant, as a visitor is often expectant in a new landscape. For me, these young piedmont woods are home base, the furniture of a deep, psychic comfort. Something lined up in me thirty years earlier when I first visited this abandoned quarry with Ab and David. When I stepped out of the truck, I felt like I was suddenly rooted again as deeply as a white oak. I wrote my first poem, "Collecting Snakes at the Abandoned Granite Quarry," after visiting this quarry. David and I caught a coachwhip on that visit, an elusive snake known for its bad temper. When I first saw the place, I passed like some insect through metamorphosis, from college student to poet, though that student poem did not make me famous, as Padgett's first novel, *Edisto*, had made him.

In the decades that followed, there were many more poems for me, but I also began writing essays—long and short—about places like this abandoned quarry. I am interested in speaking for places that have become sanctuary through neglect, abandonment, or abuse. In other words, I became interested in most of the old South—abandoned rice fields, old canals, piedmont quarries, and collapsed mountain house sites deep in recovering woods. What interests me is that I imagine and encounter creatures in these places that don't seem affected by the world closing in around them. There are snakes, lizards, salamanders, frogs, and toads living their lives untroubled—or so it seems on the surface—by the sprawl and spread of urban comfort zones. Even though populations may be endangered, individuals of a particular species are carrying on. It is in these places I have always practiced a "catch and release" sort of amateur herpetology learned in college from true scientists David and Ab, and today I'm returning to it.

At a question-and-answer session the day before, I had asked Padgett why it is that Southern writers so often set their stories in places they've made up, while his novel *Edisto* will forever be associated with a real place, a sea island down the coast from Charleston.

Padgett fielded my question and considered my notion that a real landscape and his imaginary setting might be confused, that somehow his story could be laid like a grid map or a survey over an actual island. Earlier in the session he had explained how for him the story of precocious Simons Manigault began as "an insupportable notion"—that of a fourteen-year-old writing a novel—and he had taken the notion to its extreme. If the narrative had "collapsed" early, it would have ended up a short story. But as he wrote, the notion extended itself with energy into several hundred pages, and in the end, the notion became *Edisto*, not an island but a novel.

So character and plot and setting are not to be confused with a real place? "Those people on Edisto with my book on their coffee table will be surprised if they ever read it," Padgett said in answer to my inquiry about place. "It's not Edisto. I just wanted to set it between Charleston and Savannah."

Since yesterday I have pondered Padgett's answer with the perplexed aesthetic of a personal essayist. I write about real places and people—like this granite quarry. I don't mean to make things up. I want to create a solid conceit to work from: that the world exists. In my essay work, I try to walk a ridge-top trail between imagination and reality. It's different territory than that of a fiction writer like Padgett. The drop-off for me is distinct in either direction—imagination on one side, and fact on the other. I know when I'm off the trail in either direction. The fiction writer walks always in the rich bottomland of the imagination. The trail of fact leads the writer into the imagination's thicket.

Still too early in the morning for snake catching, we walk up a very real, rain-soaked trail, once county road and now mealy asphalt softened by corrosive vines and invading grass. "It gives me great hope to see how quickly a road can be dissolved," Ab says, returning to this place after twenty years.

Padgett listens quietly to Ab's observations and David's joking with me. Ab is walking point, his binoculars suspended around his neck. David, in shorts like Padgett, cracks on me, says that he remembers only one snake we ever caught at the old quarry back in college, and so maybe I should go back and rename that first poem "Collecting *Snake* at the Abandoned Granite Quarry." I admit to him that memory is a slippery thing, the imagination stretching its constraints and pulling at reality like the roots of poison ivy vines on the road we walk.

It occurs to me that this is how real experience is transformed into art. Fiction would be easier. Change the names, let the place serve the story, make it up. Maybe ten years from now Padgett will find a way to turn this day in South Carolina into a novel, to follow the notion of us all together toward story, but for me the outing is pure nonfiction.

It was essay, a true, literary set-up, from the moment I conceived this trip.

I did not coerce Padgett to come snake hunting with us, though I did offer him money for the reading, and he might claim that I as much as promised him a very real coachwhip. If Padgett checked his field guide before boarding the plane to fly north, he might not have been very hopeful. In Spartanburg County, we are at the western limits of the snake's range.

The coachwhip David and I caught years ago had been an adult about three feet long. I remember the snake had a large, dark, fierce head, but soon, a foot down its slender explosive body, the color changed to light brown. I don't think it bit either of us. I like to think about how the creature actually looks like a coachwhip; the scales on the snake's side were so distinct that they looked like braided leather, and the head looked like a black leather handle. Is it nature's own onomatopoeia?

I know what the snake we caught over a quarter-century ago looked like because I still have a slide that I took in 1976, the snake active and cornered among pine straw and granite rip-rap on the quarry floor. The creature is kinetic, ready to jump out of the small frame. Written in my college scrawl below the image is "Coachwhip, Pacolet, SC." The date stamp by the developer tells me it had been November when we caught the snake, or maybe it was earlier, and I had been lazy getting the film developed. Facts become slippery over time.

As we walk toward the quarry, David narrates what he remembers of catching the coachwhip—how we had seen the snake sunning high on the cliff on a ledge of granite. Ab listens, and then adds that he too had seen a coachwhip at the quarry years ago, a juvenile. Padgett listens closely to this brief natural history of the quarry. It's not much to work with but a compelling introduction to this quarry, fraught with serpents.

Padgett's seen several coachwhips in his native Florida. The individuals he's seen fled just like the field guide says they would—"with a burst of speed." His comments suggest he knows their reputation for being savage fighters when cornered, and I think that is one reason he has come north. The possibility of catching the wily coachwhip is like some plot point in a story, a character just off-stage with a loaded gun— in the case of the coachwhip, a nasty set of tiny teeth.

I met Padgett at a gathering of writers in Nashville, and we struck up a conversation over dinner, not about books, but snakes and snake hunting. For some reason I thought of the quarry when we began to talk, and at that moment, I imagined bringing him here to this Spartanburg County place, a wild spot I had not seen in over twenty-five years. And soon after, I imagined asking my college friend David, and my friend and former teacher Ab, to come along as well for a snake-catching reunion. We had not been in the field together in years, but I could see the three of us walking with Padgett in the quarry, looking for snakes.

Now we are all here, five people—including David's sister—with different lives drawn together by this swift, elusive creature. As Padgett and I have literature as a mutual field of endeavor, my two old friends David and Ab have backgrounds in the science: reptile and amphibian fieldwork and wildlife biology. Betsy, David's sister, is a mountain homesteader and bronze caster and has shown up by chance.

Padgett can't help but notice this is a real place, obviously familiar to his hosts, a place of almost mythic proportions to them. I watch how he reacts. Padgett listens to stories and observations, our old field jabber. He seems intrigued with the place's possibilities. As we walk the road in, he looks at the edges, the ecotones, shifting his eyes as David and Ab do along the margins, looking for movement and shifts in patterns.

For David's sister, Betsy, the quarry floats in deep high-school memory only as a possible field trip with a legendary biology teacher. "It could have been some other quarry," she says as we walk in and approach the drop-off. Looking over into the depths she adds, "Now I'm not sure."

Padgett hasn't said much on this outing. Maybe he isn't comfortable among strangers yet. I'm sure he doesn't know exactly what to expect. I haven't figured out much about him since he arrived. We are both writers and should have some things in common, but unlike other literary visitors, he seems bored talking about his books, so I don't ask many literary questions, especially about *Edisto*. He seems more interested in talking about the quarry.

The night before, after his reading at the college and a dinner among colleagues, I had given him a ride back to the hotel. Padgett stood with the truck door open and told me not to get my hopes up about returning to this abandoned quarry after twenty-five years. Then he leaned into the cab and told me a story of how once he had tried to return to an old barrow pit of his childhood in North Florida. It was a place where he had learned to love and fear snakes. He remembered how as a child he had seen indigo snakes "crossing and recrossing the trail into the place." He said he wanted to catch them so badly he had devised a plan of throwing forked sticks at them from a great distance. "You know how when you are scared but you want something so much?"

When he finally went back and looked for the place as an adult all he found was "a new subdivision with bigger houses." Even the barrow pit was gone, and in its place "was a lake with a little island and paddle boats."

At the abandoned quarry's apex I feel lucky because I see that Padgett is wrong about this place of memory. The quarry site is still just as I remembered it from twenty-five years before. The quarry drops away, not an industrial pit with water in the bottom, but something from an earlier time of industry, a giant V carved out of an accessible hillside, like the Vietnam Memorial with trees and shattered granite on its floor.

I walk to the lip and look down sixty feet. An old stone mason in Spartanburg has told me there are broken columns cut for the state capital in Columbia from the 1860s abandoned among the stunted pines and scattered hardwoods. I hope my morning in the quarry will prove him right. Confirming this little scrap of history is something I want maybe as much as Padgett wants a coachwhip.

It is a beauty spot. I gaze from the lip of the quarry out over what must be fifteen miles of piedmont woods with the quarry sunk like an arrowhead among them. The distance seizes my perspective and grounds it like lightning at the horizon. There is power in layer upon layer of green lingering in the morning light, so rich and new and unpredictable.

Driving in, we passed the working quarry with granite dust and tractors and the gaping hole in the earth. It had been the opposite of this open sky, an engineered hole in the earth inching further outward toward valuable mysteries like this old quarry every afternoon at 3:00 P.M. when they blast more rock loose from the walls. But on the verge of the old quarry, we could be on another planet except for the occasional warning horns in the distance as the trucks back up to receive their loads of gravel to haul out to the growing county's roads.

On the quarry's parameter we walk a huge flat granite outcrop covered with moss and stained dark brown and silver with chemical weathering. We walk down its sloping surface and notice the area sprinkled with the core waste of granite drills. They are two to six inches long and caught in little pockets of moss all down the slope where the sheet wash of storm run-off has left them. They look like little columns or, as Padgett comments, "stone, round Lincoln logs." We pick them up, taking them back as paperweights.

As Padgett walks down the sloping stone he stops, his Docksiders splayed out around a clump of moss, and picks up a perfect projectile point left suspended on a column of red mud, napped from ruddy chert. The point has been broken off, but there is no mistaking the steady work of human intention and imagination on this chip of stone.

We speculate on how long this point has been lost or abandoned. Three hundred years? Three thousand? Padgett pockets the artifact, a fetish for future memory, and we walk on down the slope toward the quarry floor.

I am surprised by the richness of the rubble distributed on this huge flat of stone. My memories of trips here in college do not include this sloping expanse of rock. All I remember is the deep quarry with its dark fractured walls. I envy Padgett this stone syllable from the story of the quarry's past. Laid side-by-side with the drill corings and the beer cans abandoned on the trail, this point makes a sentence out of human occupation—aboriginal, early American, post-industrial.

The sun is highlighting the south edge of the quarry. We know it's where we should go if we want to find serpents. Ab works on down through stunted sweet gums, cedars, and pines, steps off a solid shelf of granite to the quarry's needle-softened floor where a pine had died and the stump still stands. He strips bark, looking for small snakes or salamanders that might seek shelter in the ruin. David is already walking the long line of industrial moraine that juts out from the short side of the quarry. Within moments of descent to the floor he spots a snake. "Black rat snake," he says and moves fast, catching the snake's tail before it disappears among the rubble.

We pass the snake back among us. I hold it and sharp musk rises from my hands, a smell common during my youthful snake catching. The rat snake is calm and twists about slowly. I finally pass it to Padgett who holds it too, gazing at the black, coiling wildness in his hands. "It's not a coachwhip, but we won't walk away empty-handed," I say.

"Before you go off to the middle of nowhere we better go fishing, to ratify our experience together," Simons Manigault says to his friend and mentor, Taurus, in *Edisto*. The two characters are fishing for mullet. The day before, Padgett has told an audience at Wofford College that it's the only chapter in the novel where "everything is true." He explained to the afternoon session how this scene happened and he just wrote it down, inserting Simons and Taurus in replacement for himself and a friend. Maybe fishing, the act of securing from the world its riches, is beyond fiction. As Simons says, it ratifies.

They fished, and we hunt. Holding this first snake has ratified my experience with Padgett, not the reading the night before. Not the talk of books and publishing. Here is something unpracticed and raw for two writers to exchange, something moving between us that does not need an agent. David has caught this place's long muscular center for us, and passed it along to admire and then release back into the world. Maybe that's what's strange about art. A novel or story composed and abandoned by its author never settles back into the experiential world from which it came. It remains a human artifact, like this quarry, a space utilized, a beautiful human scar upon the landscape. An essay serves a little different purpose. Often the world stays with it. They say a fact is that which can be confirmed, and personal essays are often full to the brim with facts.

At the reading the night before, *Edisto* had not been on Padgett's playlist as I had secretly hoped it would be. He had searched at the podium instead among a loose sheaf of fresh pages, stories published and unpublished, what he called "a failed novel" about Boris Yeltsin, and two short, dream-like tales entitled "South Carolina" and "Florida." The work seemed wild and elusive. The audience laughed. He commented on how uncertain he was about what he would read next. He wandered among this raw material of fiction as if a man looking for a trail into the deeper woods. After an hour, at 8:30, he stopped abruptly, thanked us for our attendance.

"That was a strange little reading," Padgett said, stepping out from behind the podium.

What we know of a place often comes from the keen eye of a naturalist, or the stories we carry away. Between the five of us there are as many answers. For another hour we explore the ridge of rubble, and Ab points out fence lizards abundant among the slabs and deadfall and speaks their scientific name, "*Sceloporus*," and places the creature within a web of his deep knowing.

Walking the high dark north wall of the quarry I spot one more snake on a bench of granite. "The mother of all hognoses," Ab calls it as we approach. Everyone walks over and admires the three-foot, relaxed eastern hognose with the distinct, turned-up snout. Padgett picks it up and holds this snake, then puts it down, triggering its defensive stance, the cobra-like spreading of neck that prompted the nonpoisonous hognose's common name, "spreading adder." Ab picks it up and explains how rarely they bite but how painful it can be if they do. There's a long tooth in the snake's throat "used to deflate toads," its primary food source.

As we leave the hognose where we found it, I comment with audible regret to Padgett that we've not seen the coachwhip or found the columns of the old capital. He puts the hognose back on its altar of granite, says he thinks that what we have experienced is actually better. We've found two snakes we could hold calmly in our hands. Padgett's right. The coachwhip remains more powerful as a hidden mystery and the abandoned capital columns as a story the stonemason believes and will continue to pass along.

Edisto is still in print, even if Padgett doesn't read from it these days. Simons Manigault now sleeps between the covers of a book decades old. Each time someone buys it, teaches it, or checks it out of the library, it's as if this bright sun has hit a sloping face of granite.

A good story is real and elusive as a coachwhip. The world lights up not suddenly from above but with brightness leaking out of a familiar landscape, from cracks and fissures in the stone. I walk on, intent on this return to the place of my youthful poetizing. Not even the trucks hauling the rock away in the distance can bring me out of the light's sudden revelry and the rediscovered wilderness of my own perception.

SOLS CREEK FALLS

One Sunday in the Southern mountains, I decide that rather than go to church I'll search for a waterfall with my friend Randy. Looking for just any waterfall in the Southern Appalachians is a little like scouting trout in a pool in a mountain stream. You know they are there, it's just that you have to train your eye to stay focused spot-to-spot, and soon you'll see them flashing by. With waterfalls it's the opposite. Your eye's moving. It's the waterfall that stays still. Driving a curving mountain back road in the high country you let your eye move along the ridgelines and creek draws until sooner or later a waterfall will cross your vision.

But looking for a particular waterfall, like the one up Sols Creek, is a little harder. Many times the good ones (and I've been told this is one of the best) are high up in the deepest grooves of a crazy gorge, a place where even the trails lead into wildness and doubt, where you turn and look out and see something startling.

The sublime doesn't exist down South. Whatever true wildness was once found from Virginia to Georgia has been bleached out of the landscape, the sublime draining through the cracks of civilization and settlement. Maybe Mark Catsby or William Bartram wandered some true wilderness that would rival Wyoming, but today the Southern Appalachian backcountry is checkerboarded with condominium developments, church camps and patchy wood lots. So goes the argument.

"Sols Creek?" Randy asks when I mention a plan to go find the waterfall I'd been told is the wildest place in the South. Randy's an expert paddler, a river guide, an old friend from Spartanburg and a classmate from the 1970s at Wofford College. He's been to Sols Creek Falls once. He tells the story of clambering up on a little grassy knoll below the waterfall to drink some wine he'd hauled in, looking up only to see two goats with curving horns clambering along the cliffs next to the waterfall. Of course, they weren't mountain goats, only feral escapees from some mountain farm, but it was enough to make Randy think twice about time and space, to wonder whether he had slipped through some crevice into some real Western wilderness sublime.

On my map I can see how Sols Creek wanders eight miles off the high flank of Rich Mountain, its headwaters almost on the summit, just south of the highest stretch of the Blue Ridge Parkway, a country so far up in the air that it feels like Colorado or Montana even in the middle of a North Carolina July.

Right above Bear Creek Reservoir the creek crosses Highway 281, the only hardtop for ten miles, and drops three hundred feet a mile through contours suggesting a classic mountain creek gorge. Randy assures me that less than a mile upstream from where Sols Creek turns turbid and green and disappears under the waters of Bear Creek Reservoir, it takes one of the most sublime plunges in North Carolina. There is a "rock amphitheater" where an ancient hemlock log is magically balanced between two boulders, a plunge pool deep enough to swim in, and standing tulip poplars ten feet thick at the base.

We head out on Sunday morning. Highway 281 crawls up out of the hamlet of Tuckaseegee and follows the river for four or five miles just to the north of Cedar Cliff Reservoir where the state road begins to climb steadily into some of the highest, wildest country in the east. At one time prior to the 1930s, the Tuckaseegee was wild too, with rapids, moods, and a spring attitude like a mountain bear.

Circling on intuition, we miss the access road to Bear Creek and drive ten miles too far, all the way to the last of three lakes on the upper Tuckaseegee, Wolf Creek.

"I wanted to see this country anyway," Randy says, making me feel better for my lack of attention.

After we cross the high dam at Wolf Creek and see 281 turn to gravel, we stop a local man walking along the road and ask about Bear Creek. His gait is natural and prolonged. He is thin as a ghost, wearing a mountaineer's flop hat, and has milky blue Celtic eyes straight out of the Iron Age. He listens, reluctantly gives directions, and we turn and head back down the mountain.

The access lot at Bear Creek Reservoir is full of 4x4s and empty boat trailers when we finally pull up. We have the only roof racks on the property. Paddle power has never had much clout, I'm sure, on Bear Creek.

Neither one of us is happy with the canoe we have been forced by timing to paddle across the lake, a tandem white-water boat with a bow described by the manufacturer as a "bruise water." We have little hope of making much time pushing across the lake, but Sols Creek is somewhere up the lake, and not very often in a pilgrimage do the pilgrims have everything they need or want. What would be the point? Part of the plan is finding your way at the appropriate speed. Chaucer knew all about this.

We take the canoe off the Trooper, load a little gear—paddles, life jackets, food and a jug of water—and carry our vessel to the boat launch. My dog, Ellie Mae, follows, uncertain what we are up to with that long boat. I've never had her in a canoe before, but figure I'll baptize her in Sols Creek, and she'll be a canoe dog forever.

After the obligatory rude powerboater entry into the lake (a bass boat nearly runs us over on the ramp as we are loading gear, as if the canoe did not qualify as a water-craft) we take our first few strokes and begin bobbing across the green water. We are sitting on paddling thwarts, not seats, and our knees are tucked under the seats white-water style. "I'm too old for this," Randy says. "My knees feel like rusty hinges."

Ellie Mae is riding fine and quiet in the small space between the two of us. We have to adjust our paddle strokes a little to avoid her nose, which she keeps ceaselessly to the gunnels as if to get a fix on her position by the smell of the lake's surface. A beagle-basset is not a water dog, but Ellie Mae accommodates to the slight embarrassment just fine. She looks much more comfortable when we spot a poodle on the bow of a passing bass boat.

After a thirty-minute paddle and one or two false starts up a wrong cove, Randy says, "Now this looks more like waterfall country." The walls of the valley are rising more abruptly, and there is visible rock among the trees, and even an occasionally sheer cliff of dark granite. We are following the course of the submerged riverbed, and I imagine the old wild river and the rapids below. I am haunted by the ghost of a drowned river below the surface of a reservoir; but down there, it comforts me to think the current's ancient flow is silted away for some future day of judgment when the temporal dam shows its age, and the river emerges again.

On Bear Creek Reservoir we are only ten miles west of the Tennessee Valley divide, but from there west to the Mississippi the saying from 1930 until the present was, "If the flow's good, dam it." The government built dams at Thorpe Reservoir, Nantahala Lake, Fontana, Santeelah, the infamous Tellico with its ancient Cherokee burial grounds and snail darter. Almost everywhere there was gradient in these mountains, the hand of TVA passed over a wild river and killed it dead in its ancient bed.

It's seems the height of human greed and indecency to kill a wild river for political, recreational, and real estate purposes. I know it's mostly a "power" trip, pumping out the watts for North Carolina's ten million summer air conditioners. TVA would say, "If God would had the money, he'da air conditioned the South."

But the Bear Creek impoundment is pretty, the way a poodle can be pretty. It has a few houses on it, and the fishermen are friendly in a general way as devoted users. It's only the jet skis, the horseflies of lake recreation, for which I can muster quite as much hate as I hold for professional river killers. Randy tells me that even white-water rivers are not safe from the roar and slashing turns of the jet skis. "Out in Oregon they are taking them up Class II and III rivers," he explains. "They've already had to outlaw jet boats on the Colorado."

With each paddle stroke, I hear the modern world closing in around me, and I feel powerless against it as I dip my paddle into the water. I remember arguing once about snowmobiles out west with a friend. "They should be banned in all but a few areas," I said.

"What's wrong with snowmobiles?" she said. "They're fun, and people love them. Everyone loves them but you and your eco-nut friends."

"They pollute an entire area when they're there where you are cross-country skiing."

"They meet the government standards for emission."

"I mean noise. You can hear them for ten miles."

"Oh, noise! You think noise is pollution? That's a pretty extreme position."

"Of course noise is pollution."

"You've got a choice. Just don't listen."

Bear Lake is drawn down ten feet, and we stop on an exposed sand beach to stretch our legs and let the dog touch dry land. There is a fire ring of broken rock with a dozen beer cans bent, burnt, and abandoned. The beach sand is lousy with silver dollar-size scraps of mica, and I remember a tomb I've seen in a mound in Ohio, Adena Culture, and how the corpses were interned with mica sheets big as pie plates as a ceremonial covering. The mica was acquired in trade from tribes in the Southern Appalachians. On the beach at Bear

Creek, each piece of mica mirrors my sadness for the drowned Tuckaseegee.

While we are stopped, Ellie runs along the water's edge where wave wash makes a strange noise she's never heard before, snapping at the incoming waves and barking. I see her as a canine Hamlet, taking arms against my lake of troubles.

Back in the canoe, we pass an island in the channel where a houseboat is moored, and two dogs run the beach and bark as we make a sharp left. We begin a short paddle up the narrowing confluence of Sols Creek. The powerboat in front of us pulls in for an instant, pivots, and then throttles back out into the main lake.

"They're looking at something," Randy says. We drift, and at exactly the moment when our canoe lines up with the entering creek's last small cataract we see the top of Sols Creek Falls, maybe a quarter mile up the rocky creek and one hundred feet above the lake's surface. "Yep, this is waterfall country."

We find the best way to approach Sols Creek Falls is to say a quick prayer to the god of free flow and wade upstream from the first tiny rapid though an enclosing snarl of blooming rhododendron, shattered slabs of granite, and cold creek water, boulders fallen into creases, fans, spouts, showers and pools.

The space quickly grows charged with the ions of wildness with each one hundred feet of falling water we put behind us. The Sols Creek Falls is up there somewhere, maybe beyond the next cataract and we are headed right for it. The creek is quiet in the way impossibly agitated water in a mountain stream is quiet. I slip once and scrape my calf on a rock and bleed a little. Randy has on his huge brimmed farmer's hat and is easy to spot in the shadows and mist. We both have on white water sandals and are wading in the deep fonts of cold creek water sometimes up to our waists. The dog quickly has that wet dog look, but she boulder-hops upstream toward whatever is pulling her dog's will over the boulders.

John Lane

I know it's overdone, but the creek name alone (pronounced "souls") prods me to pull out the old cliché that deep mountain forests with wild water running through them can be compared to cathedrals. Well, it's true: that's why it is and remains a cliché. Clichés are in some essential way the truest truths our language has to offer. The forest in a place like the tiny gorge below Sols Creek Falls is awe-inspiring, like a cathedral, and strangely out of place and time. Who on this busy Sunday on a mountain lake would make the difficult pilgrimage up Sols Creek to see the waterfall? Everyone else within a square mile is fishing or sunning on their houseboat when paradise is less than an hour away.

We eat our sandwiches at the base of Sols Creek Falls, and, yes, there is that magic log. I'll come back sometime with another sandwich, navigating the next pilgrimage a little more on faith and less on the first timer's intuition. As a famous Hindu scholar once said, "The best things cannot be spoken of, and the next best are misunderstood." Suffice it to say that the Sols Creek Falls is sublime; it's out there, just off the path the bass boats motor along.

REDEMPTION ECOLOGY

We are on the Georgia coast, Ossabaw Island, for a short weekend to talk about Southern nature. There are ten writers—Janisse Ray, Ann Fisher-Wirth, Franklin Burroughs, Thomas Rain Crowe, Melissa Walker, Jan DeBlieu, Susan Cerulean, Barbara Ras, and Dorinda Dallmeyer—and one artist and activist, Raven Burchard.

We're taking about big issues—species diversity, wild places, democracy, our own spiritual lives, "writing in place." It's Saturday morning, and we're sitting in a prefab hunting lodge brought on a barge to this sea island off the Georgia coast in the 1890s. A big old-fashioned wood fire heats up the living room. We burn live oak, lots of it, piled on the porch outside the back door by the staff of the Ossabaw Island Foundation.

There are only three hours to discuss everything that concerns us, and then we will walk to the marsh side of the island, to a place called Cane Patch. Six of us have new books coming out, texts that will project this group's ideas and perceptions about nature and culture in the South deeper into regional and national consciousness, books about bays and swamps and rivers, and endangered birds, and, as is Jan DeBlieu's case, even the stars. Everyone has something to report—prizes won, landscapes explored or defended, conferences organized. We are all deeply engaged—as writers, activists, human beings.

This is our third time on Ossabaw, and seven years have separated this visit and the first. Two previous pilgrimages we stayed a mile further east in "the big house," a mansion built in 1926 by the Torrey family, industrialists from the North who'd bought the whole island as a hunting preserve near the turn of the last century and, by way of their investment, saved it from coastal sprawl. Sandy West, the surviving Torrey on the island, still lives in the mansion. Late in the afternoon she will have us down for tea. We are part of Sandy's vision for the place, from 1961 to the present. She always wanted artists and thinkers to retreat to Ossabaw to explore, create, and connect.

"Public policy, public land, and public environmental education—it doesn't seem to be working anymore," Janisse Ray offers to start off our conversation. "Global capitalism, the loss of democracy, the rise of the religious Right— can we start the change from here?"

These are tough questions for tough times. We are all despairing in some way—mourning the loss of election campaigns, of conservation battles. Melissa Walker says she has given up on Georgia, her home state, after the loss of a key battle for wilderness on Cumberland Island. Ann Fisher-Wirth talks of Oxford, Mississippi's failed battle against a Wal-Mart. Thomas Crowe describes a five-thousand-acre "gated community" constructed in the wild reaches of the Southern mountains where he lives. I am more hopeful, describing how I have dug in on an impaired piedmont creek and am doing what I can to restore some sense of hope in the upcountry of South Carolina. "I'm studying the Archaic— ten thousand years ago—to find out about the patterns where we live," I say. By "Archaic," I mean a period of classification that archeologists give to human history from 8,000 B.C. to 1,000 B.C.E.

"The retreat to the archaic. It begins one spirit at a time," is what Franklin Burroughs offers after I've made my statement. Frank says he is quoting Faulkner's "The Bear." By archaic, Frank is using Faulkner to talk about those Choctaw "Indian times" that are still present in "The Bear" within the living character and the morals and values and the actions of a character named Sam Fathers. Because Frank is by nature skeptical, he makes it clear he isn't sure whether Faulkner would consider the retreat to the archaic a good thing. After all, we live in communities, and half of us are teachers, present or past. I offer how maybe "advance into the future one student at a time" is a better strategy.

"But so many college age people are essentially dead, hopeless…for them everything is either forbidden or success oriented. What they think they're supposed to do is march straight ahead," Ann says. "Everybody has a vocation and a central nature. Affirm it."

"Even the old Robber Barons were somehow moderated," Dorinda Dalmeyer chimes in from across the room. "We need visionaries. Once there was John Muir and Teddy Roosevelt."

"We can't forget the war in Iraq," Raven says from a table outside the circle, and we all agree.

"What we're after is a better life," Barbara Ras says. "It's all about interconnection, ecology."

"My instincts are for withdrawal into the local, things of the spirit, and indulgence of my own shyness," Frank adds. "But utopian community will not get us very far."

Someone brings up our lost writer friend James Kilgo, here with us for the first two gatherings but now dead, and how he believed that the only way to save the South's wildlands was through Southern churches. Frank agrees, though he adds he is not an active church-goer: "The loss of history and the loss of the texture of history. We're all concerned about that. You can't write the Bible out—the writers we admire are always only one step away from it. I think that we are first and foremost writers, even when we are our most literal and most concerned about, say, the swallowtail kite. It's all ultimately metaphoric—and it's a complex web. The Bible offers us an arsenal of rhetoric. Let us use it."

This discussion of the Bible and Southern religion makes some of us uncomfortable. "What the hell is Jesus?" Thomas asks as the discussion veers and probes into this only territory of the conversation that many on the mainland would find relevant among all our topics.

"If we're going to win this battle we need to win it with the truth," Jan adds. "We need to redefine ourselves not as environmentalists but as citizens, and we need to speak the truth."

But what is the truth for an environmental writer? As Frank suggests, our power comes from language. As I listen, I remember something a religion professor friend of mine once said in conversation: "If the environmentalism movement has failed, it's probably for the same reason all fundamentalisms fail. Environmentalism often looks back instead of forward. It's often failed to embrace modernity." I also remember what my friend said when I explained about environmentalism's metaphor of "restoration," as in "restoration ecology."

"Maybe," he suggested, "environmentalists should try redemption instead of restoration. You know, accept the damage that's been done and then try to overcome it for some common good."

Can writing redeem an ecosystem? An island? Redeem means literally, in the Latin, "to buy back, to purchase," as the Torrey family did for Ossabaw nearly one hundred years ago, so when we use it we can, at least unconsciously, tie clearly to those bottom line metaphors that flourish all around us. But there is also in the word "redeem" a suggestion of freedom, reform, reclamation, rescue, and, yes, even restoration. Redeem is actually quite a multi-purpose word, though when I say it the feel of the rhetoric somehow always remains religious. Maybe that's not a bad thing around people who talk of having time "only for eternal matters." Redemption ecology rather than restoration ecology—maybe that's what good Southern environmentalists can practice.

The talk continues to circulate among us for three hours. We burn with a holy fire. We are our own little community for two nights, and we take our place in a grand tradition on Ossabaw. For forty years, the Ossabaw Foundation had brought people here to think, bond, sort, bicker, imagine, and cleave asunder. For forty-eight hours, we form our own tribe circling around the ceremonial fire.

How do we begin "one spirit at a time," which in Faulkner somehow includes both humans and bears? This is the central question that keeps coming up all day on the island: how can we as a people continue to tell a story—in our churches and our families in particular—where our needs as "God's creatures" remain central to the planet, a story that, so far, has lead to air pollution, loss of habitat for all other species, the worst habits of globalization, and major demographic stress. How do we learn to follow the plot of another complex story that includes evolution and geologic time and biodiversity and E. O. Wilson's "biophilia" as central themes and plot elements?

"Among a few thinkers the conception of prehistory has changed, perhaps to the extent of a paradigm shift. Natural history, paleo-anthropology, and forager research empirically validate the hypothesis that humankind is an unfinished project whose roots extend into a fertile soil far beneath ancient Sumeria and Egypt," Max Oelschlaeger says in *The Idea of Wilderness*:

> The picture of Paleolithic culture is changing dramatically as a result. Scholars are sketching an affirmative profile of Paleolithic humans, defining them in terms of positive, shared attributes rather than differences... our prehistoric ancestors lived well by hunting and foraging; they buried human remains and were religious; they had an understanding of nature's ways that reflects an intelligence equal to our own.... In short, Paleolithic people were not the ignorant, fierce brutes that civilized humans imagine, a fact that places the onus upon us—to reassess our self-concept. We come from that green world of the hunter-gatherers.

We "come from that green world," and when we return to Ossabaw we reoccupy it for a moment. We see in visits like ours that to reflect back on the hunter-gathering culture of the Paleo or Archiac periods is to leap and leave behind that inadequate narrative of "the cradle of civilization." The "fertile crescent" alone is not all we need to discover the source of our humanness. We need a redemptive story that reaches back much further into human prehistory, a story only archeologists and anthropologists can help us form—all the way to foraging and hunting and soapstone and seasonal camping culture that looks much more like a weekend trip onto Ossabaw than it does a trip to Disneyworld. What would this story look like with equal parts God Almighty and spirits of the land? That's a question we keep asking on the island.

Thomas Berry is a Southerner whose book *The Great Work* has articulated "the earth story." Berry is somehow able to move human beings out of the center and, in the spirit of Teilhard de Chardin, and place all creation there. Berry calls the earth "the garden planet," and last weekend on Ossabaw Island we all saw clearly what he means. We were guests on a huge sea island approached only by boat (or a damn long swim) where there are only ten or so "resident" humans. Even though there are roads and buildings and 500 years of European and 10,000 years of human occupation, there is still a sense on Ossabaw that the balance is closer to right.

But humans are like ink in a glass of water. Just a drop colors the whole glass over time. Still, it is indeed "the garden" on the island. After talking around the fire, we "retreat" to the archaic when a group of us walks out to an ancient shell mound on the marsh side of the island. We saunter along a dirt two-track through big pines and the sweeping limbs of live oaks. The marsh is to our north, and the air is cool. After a fifteen-minute walk through the forest we come to the shell mound, what was the seasonal campsite for an archaic band of native peoples, a six-foot tall midden of oyster and periwinkle and conch shells deposited over generations of occupation.

I'm always transformed and transported when I sit in such places and ponder what little we know of these ancient cousins. I feel the peace of their lives. I know all the downsides—diseases and relatively short lives—but what we know tells us that these people lived lives not at all like Hobbes's "short and brutal" existences.

Frank, Susan, Dorinda, and I explore the back reaches of the site. I find one shard of pottery, a reminder to me of the lives led here. We also come upon a patch not of cane but of red buckeye ready to bloom in the late February chill. The pale green leaves are soft and tender. Buckeye, a showy native plant, comes to life early, with eight-inch spikes of coral flowers that the humming birds love. The blooms are close to unfurling but not quite out. Another pilgrim will have to enjoy their color later in the month. But the buckeye is not all beauty. The stems, seeds, and flowers of the plant are poisonous, and the native people who lived in the islands probably crushed the branches and seeds and threw them into pools of water to stun fish. When the fish rose to the surface, they were easily caught. Settlers later used the gummy roots as a soap substitute and for home remedies made from the bitter bark. I think how we finally will all be native when we learn the land in such an intimate way.

Environmentalists have always known that the land is the best place to go for our metaphors, and I struggle to hold onto the red buckeye as metaphor—buckeye as stunning beauty that sustains? Buckeye as early food for the hummingbirds? Buckeye as redeemer of winter, buying spring back with early blooms?

On the walk back from Cane Patch several in the group listen for pine warblers in the big loblollies; two others watch as a river otter fishes in a tidal creek. Thomas Berry says we all now need to enter "the Ecozoic," a period where humans are "a mutually beneficial presence on the Earth." And that future can exist only when "we understand the universe as composed of subjects to be communed with, not as objects to be exploited. 'Use' as our primary relationship with the planet must be abandoned." Berry sees how difficult this will be. After all, the people who lived thousands of years at Cane Patch loved the buckeye both for its beauty and for its utility—its use.

I feel the cold and rain. My visits to the Ossabaw have worked as a path to redemption. When I come across the water by boat, I abandon my need for bridges and accept the help of others. I trust the idea of public land for a few days to keep me in a state close to wildness.

ReGenesis

Mixing pleasure with curiosity I set out on a Sunday morning in late October with some friends to paddle a three-mile stretch of Fairforest Creek just outside the city limits of Spartanburg, South Carolina. Four of us will put in on South Liberty Street in Arkwright, an old mill village, and take out a few hours later downstream on the 295 bypass. This will be urban boating at its best. Fairforest Creek is not a wilderness: it drains most of Spartanburg's south side industrial zones—small-time machine shops, distribution plants, even a large petroleum tank farm just downstream from where we'll take out. The Fairforest is not blue ribbon water for anything—fish, recreation, or scenery. It's a working class creek and DHEC, South Carolina's regulatory agency, classifies it "impaired," a word a friend once pointed out tells us little about the stream but loads about our relationship with it.

In spite of the less-than-pristine nature of the creek, I've convinced my companions, GR, his teenage son Phillip, and Gerald, that a morning on the water—any water—is worth it. Paddling pleasure is not hard to come by once the boat's in the current, even on the Fairforest, though the water's low, the result of a record dry fall many are quick to blame on global warming. Pleasure aside, the curiosity is easier to explain and appreciate. As we're loading the boats, I tell my friends that what I'm really interested in is claiming what may be "a first descent" through the territory of "ReGenesis," Spartanburg's national poster child for environmental justice, an EPA-cited brownfield and two Superfund sites, what ReGenesis founder and local environmental activist Harold Mitchell called "the Devil's Triangle" when he brought attention to this industrial neighborhood in the late 1990s. Arkwright, primarily a low-income African-American community, has fought for almost a decade now to clean up the horrors of an abandoned fertilizer factory, an old textile mill with leaking chemical storage tanks, and a 30-acre city dump containing industrial and medical wastes. ReGenesis was formed for this struggle. Its story, and the story of Harold Mitchell its founder, is so compelling that in 2002 the EPA gave Mitchell its National Citizens Involvement Award, known informally as the "Erin Brockovich award." Since then ReGenesis has become a national model program for cleaning up low-income communities all over the country.

Several weeks before, Harold Mitchell had visited the humanities/biology learning community I co-teach with a toxicologist, so I'm still full of the ReGenesis story. Mitchell, fresh off a victory in a Democratic primary for the South Carolina House of Representatives, had lunch with us, visited class, and then drove us around the ReGenesis Project site in a van, giving me perspective on the story that Gerald, GR, and Phillip don't have. Though they live just up the hill in the middle-class neighborhood called Duncan Park, the nearby ReGenesis Project is mostly unknown to them.

Before we launch, I reveal one more wrinkle in the Sunday morning story. I lived in Arkwright for a year in the early 1960s, when the village was still mostly white mill workers. I was seven years old when my mother moved us there, and I have a few clear memories: eating figs off a fig tree in our backyard, which sloped down to Fairforest Creek, and going with my uncles to the nearby dump to shoot rats spotlighted amidst the rubble. When we turn down the street near where I'd lived, the creek is at the bottom of the hill. "It's so quiet here," Gerald says.

At 9:45 A.M. we unload the boats from GR's old green pickup next to the mill site. I've e-mailed Harold to warn him that if he gets reports of white guys in a fleet of old canoes headed southeast into terra incognito he'll know it's us. When we had visited the site earlier, Harold had explained how by the middle 90s the old mill had become crime-central with drugs and prostitution, and the only alternative seemed to be to clear it out and start anew. A few houses and families would stay, but mostly the ReGenesis vision was one of "renewal," a word that mostly white people had used to level the African-American community further north on Liberty Street in the 1970s. I could only hope folks had learned a great deal more about renewal since then.

On a literal level, this corner of Spartanburg clearly needs cleaning up. We drag the boats through busted bottles, old wire, and loose trash and put in at a little bold tributary running from under the old mill outflow pipe, rusted and unused for decades. Behind us on the hilltop loom several huge piles of old wood from the teardown of the mill. ReGenesis now owns the property, and Mitchell told our class that bricks and timbers are stored at the back of the site in hopes they can be reused to build a project headquarters or an ecology center someday. DHEC has approved a huge bonfire, a controlled burn, for later in the year to get rid of all the old ruined timber, the lumber with paint painstakingly sorted from the raw wood to make sure ReGenesis doesn't add more toxic waste to the air and water of Arkwright.

Finally we're on the water. There are three canoes and a small kayak mirrored on the dark surface, a flotilla that almost overwhelms the narrow space of the silted-in Arkwright millpond. Gerald and young Phillip head downstream and I paddle with GR a little ways upstream under the bridge. I want to commune for a moment with the epicenter of Arkwright, a community that makes up one of the most complex strands of my place-based DNA. I know from our class discussion of Lake Conestee, the similar old textile site in Greenville, that the toxic industrial chemicals trapped below me in the millpond sediment could possibly perplex a graduate toxicology seminar, and so instead I fix on some of

Spartanburg's old granite curbstones, now pressed into service to keep the shore from washing out under the bridge. I point them out to GR and note that they are an adaptive reuse of a local resource from quarry stone to curbstone, to rip rap, to historic curiosity in one hundred years. GR, a nature photographer when he's not teaching physiology at the college, is more interested in the way the early morning light bounces off the greasy surface of the water and settles on the bottom side of the concrete bridge in interesting patterns. As GR gets his camera out I'm reminded there is beauty around us in the world, in spite of what we do to extinguish it.

We head downstream to catch up with Gerald and Phillip. There's a large kudzu field on river left and the eroded, littered slope of the mill site on our right. Gerald's already birding. Sociology professor by day, writer and naturalist by evening, he has his binoculars out, and his true passion for the natural world is in full display. He's left the ugliness of Arkwright behind him. We've only been on the water five minutes but by sight and call Gerald's already identified a dozen species. He repeats the names and I write them all down—eastern phoebe, song sparrow, white-throated sparrow, great blue heron, crows, blue jays, kinglet, rufus-sided towhee, kingfisher, and mallards. "The mallard is the only duck that quacks," Gerald says, and I tell him he sounds a little too much like a science teacher, but I write his fun fact down anyway. For a moment, Gerald's ornithological fact serves as a finger in the dike of ugliness surrounding me as we float through the endless tunnel of kudzu.

We round another bend, and a strong odor of sewage envelopes us. It's coming from a tributary entering the mill pond from our left. I know that this small creek, unnamed on our topographical map, if explored to its headwaters, rises only a few hundred yards off of Spartanburg's Main Street, parallels Liberty Street, and empties here amidst the tires and kudzu. In its short two-mile run, it drains some of the poorest areas of the

Southside—government housing, shotgun shacks that have somehow survived into the twenty-first century, mean streets, and vacant lots full of syringe needles and malt-liquor cans. This morning there's no denying the elements of what academics and government pundits call "environmental justice" as I look up the small stream—poverty, racism, ignorance, denial, outright criminal neglect by the community's rich and powerful. It all drains into Fairforest Creek. I turn my face to avoid the smell.

We paddle on around another bend. The creek looks dead, a green fur coat of algae on everything hidden just below the surface—railroad ties, an old shopping cart, a City of Spartanburg plastic garbage can, a quarter of aluminum siding. "Gerald can have the birds," GR jokes as we head on downstream. "I'll keep the fish list today."

Old tires are everywhere. Downstream, the half-circles of four upright radials sunk in sediment look like a headless river monster in the glare. As the horizon line comes into sight where the creek drops eight feet over the concrete dam, four wood ducks shoot overhead like cruise missiles. "Oh, look," I say. "We've already had our 'wood duck moment.'"

Nobody knows what I mean, so as we beach our boats to figure out a way around the dam I explain my nature joke, how a few years ago in an environmental literature class I'd asked my students to come up with a master list of what elements every nature essay has to contain. "At least one profound wood duck moment," one smart-ass student had suggested after reading Annie Dillard's *Pilgrim at Tinker Creek* and Franklin Burroughs's *The River Home*.

Smart-ass or not, my student had been right. There's something about the flight overhead of wood ducks that seems to fit our idea of a nature essay so much better than the slow ghostly dance of blue-green algae on a twisted shopping cart thrown off a south Spartanburg bridge years before. A heavily impacted urban creek like the Fairforest has about as much in common with Tinker Creek as a wolf would to a pit bull chained to a trailer. So why not write about nature with the brief (in geologic time) brutal pageant of human use as the backdrop rather than the contested history of wildness and beauty?

This struggle of wild and tame, raw and baked, green and paved is all around us in nature writing, and not until recently did urban nature began to show up as a protagonist in the story. As I drag my boat through the kudzu and broken bottles to portage the dam, I notice "wild" native river birch and box elder reaching for sun out over what's not silted of the pond. "See, there's even wildness here," I say to Gerald. "Isn't it strange that just upstream from a government certified toxic wasteland, I'm pulled toward dreams of wild restoration?" Gerald brings up eco-critic William Cronin whose ideas would complicate my hopes of wildness as the myth of some untransformed landscape that exists somewhere else.

But I'm not willing to give up on wildness and beauty and such. Surely there's hope here for what's wild to creep upward through the poor South Side toward the inner reaches of the city, like fingers of green clutching at the urban heart.

Gerald's more bothered, as we portage our canoes around the dam, by what I've told him of Harold Mitchell's dream. Mitchell wants to "renew" the community partially by turning the flood plain below the mill site into a golf course or tidy green space with paved trails and landscaping provided by the University of Virginia's renowned landscape architecture department.

"A damn golf course? Why is it that rich white men always see golf courses as the answer to everything?" he asks. It's obvious Gerald doesn't know that Harold Mitchell is neither white nor rich. When I tell him Mitchell is an African American, the golf course seems even more absurd to him. With Gerald's mistake, I realize that there are people in

Washington, DC, who know more about Arkwright and ReGenesis than Gerald, someone who lives just up the hill.

We clear the dam, and I comment on how the old settlement of Arkwright will remain upstream of us now all the way to 295-Bypass. From our topo, we can see what's left is wooded country with no houses, maybe one thousand acres or more of raw land, much of it in a one-hundred-year flood zone. Renew or restore? With the terrible truth of Arkwright's history behind us and the vision of a golf course clouding our ideas of wilderness restoration for this flood plain, we get back into our canoes and head downstream, bumping over a few exposed rocks and rubble of construction debris left below the dam. I haven't done a very good job of explaining ReGenesis to my friends, and so I take the next mile or so to bring them up to speed.

The headwaters of the ReGenesis story is Harold Mitchell who grew up "across the tracks" from where we are now paddling, just south of the old Arkwright mill village. The day I met Mitchell at Wofford, he walked toward us from the visitors parking lot. Mitchell looked to be in his early forties, of medium build, nicely dressed in a tie and striped shirt, beautiful black pointy shoes, silver and black glasses, sporting a neatly trimmed beard. As he approached, I noticed Mitchell had his cell phone in his left hand and an earphone in his right ear. "You wouldn't believe who he gets calls from," a friend who knows him well had told me. Was he talking to someone out there in his global environmental justice network?

At lunch, Mitchell told a story that illustrated the opportunities his success with ReGenesis has opened to him and how much political savvy he's developed running in the environmental justice circles. He'd been invited to serve on the US delegation at the World Sustainable Development Conference in Johannesburg, South Africa, in September 2002, and he was at a cocktail party with all the big shots—Hillary Clinton and others. The anti-American sentiment was high, and Harold picked it up right away. He said he'd turned his nametag around in order to avoid detection as a member of the US delegation. When the Africans came up to ask him where he was from, he said in a very brusk tone with the hint of an accent, "I am from Arkwright," as if his small mill town were a kingdom. Where? "Arkwright. I am from Arkwright!"

So what about Mitchell's Arkwright has made it what several sources call a worldwide model for environmental justice? It's a complex and intriguing story, part *A Civil Action*, part *To Kill a Mockingbird*. Back home after college in 1991, Mitchell contracted a mysterious illness. He lost a great deal of weight, and the doctors considered kidney, colon, and prostate cancer. After a series of tests, the doctors couldn't find out what was wrong and Mitchell wanted answers. "Just tell me I'm dying of something," he told doctors.

During the same period Mitchell was sick, his father died from a mysterious ailment. One day, looking out the window of the family home, Mitchell began to wonder if the illnesses in his household could be connected to the abandoned IMC fertilizer plant that had operated across the street from 1910 to 1986. IMC Global is the largest producer and supplier of concentrated phosphate and potash fertilizer in the world. They'd sold the old plant site to a businessman in Gaffney, South Carolina, after IMC shut it down in 1986, and in the middle 90s it was still being used for storing textile supplies.

Mitchell wondered if living so close to a fertilizer factory could make you sick. He knew his street had stayed on well water because city water was too expensive to bring in from across the tracks. Could that be a problem? He also began to ask neighbors about their medical histories and discovered quickly there was a very high incidence of cancer in his neighborhood—sixteen cases of cancer on his street alone. There were only five or six families so it made the survey quite easy. At this point Mitchell didn't know anything about "cancer clusters," but so much illness in one community seemed odd.

In the late 90s, Mitchell recovered his heath and was living in nearby Greer, working as a teacher, but he was still looking into the neighborhood fertilizer plant back home. Oddly enough, the South Carolina DHEC had certified the plant clean when it closed in 1986, but what Mitchell was hearing from the plant's neighbors did not jive with what was appearing in DHEC's files. On one of Mitchell's visits to the DHEC office, a clerk mistakenly handed him a fat file to take home, and it confirmed his worst fears of what sort of chemicals and potential waste had accumulated at the IMC plant for almost one hundred years. He began to read, ask questions of government officials, and explore all the possible ways the plant could be contaminating the area he'd grown up in.

In 1997, a DHEC survey of the neighborhood did not put Mitchell's fears to rest, though once again the agency found no contaminants. Mitchell was relentless. What we now call "environmental justice" meant little to him then, but he pushed forward simply because he wanted to find out if there was some reason why he and his neighbors were so sick.

In 1998, Mitchell tired of going it alone. It was the beginning of his remarkable ability to build partnerships and consensus. He formed a small grassroots group in Arkwright to begin to organize the information the neighbors were gathering. Mitchell began to get threatening phone calls. "You crazy nigger," an unknown caller would say when he answered his phone. "You don't need to be asking all these questions."

What could possibly be the matter with asking questions about the closed IMC fertilizer factory? In South Carolina's "pro-business environment," low or lax government regulation had always been—along with a strong anti-union past that guaranteed low wages for workers and higher profit margins for stockholders—the honey that drew out-of-state development. Mitchell began to realize that industrial pollution, dumping, and the siting of the dirtiest of the industries in black and poor neighborhoods was one of South Carolina's dark secrets.

One morning Mitchell had an unexpected visit from a representative of the South Carolina Militia. The man stood on Harold Mitchell's porch and calmly told him that the questions the budding investigator was asking were very dangerous, and that he should consider driving various routes to and from Greer when going to Arkwright to do his research.

The man seemed to know everything about him. The militia member said the Arkwright inquiry could challenge the very business establishment of the state. "Don't trust anything from the state level," he said. "Go straight to the feds." Was this guy friend or foe? It was a little confusing. When Mitchell thought of the militia he imagined those skinheads in Montana. Then he gave Mitchell the 800 number to call the EPA. Before he left the man pulled a handgun out of a holster behind his back. "He's told me all this, and now he's going to shoot me," Mitchell had told my class he thought as the gun appeared. "Do you have a permit to carry one of these?" the man asked. "If you don't, you need to get one."

Mitchell called the EPA and on the day before the agency was supposed to inspect the fertilizer plant, the owner brought in bulldozers and caved the building in, making it impossible to do an easy inspection. Mitchell filmed the demolition with his video camera, part of a long record of the project he has assembled on tape. In 1999, Harold presented all the information he'd gathered at a community meeting. DHEC stopped the owner from destroying any more of the evidence as a result.

The EPA then sent an inspector from the Atlanta office, and he walked around the site as Mitchell followed him with the video camera. The inspector dismissed everything, downplayed it all. Undaunted by this roadblock at the regional level, Mitchell used a high-school connection to convince US Senator Fritz Hollings to get involved in the Arkwright case. Hollings's chief of staff was Mitchell's former center on the Spartanburg High School football team in the mid-80s. Mitchell called his old friend, and Hollings became interested in the Arkwright case and requested an EPA investigation of the IMC site.

The third EPA inspection revealed that sulfur had been dumped over the back fence of the fertilizer company. There was a small visible yellow pile of it on the slope going down to the creek. Once the area was explored extensively, inspectors discovered there was twenty tons of sulfur in the area. There was also an abandoned acid factory underneath it as well.

"With seepage velocity of forty-six-feet per year there was no doubt all this was affecting the creek," Harold had explained to us when I visited the site with my class. The inspection also revealed an abandoned waste pond on the site where EPA estimated 1.3 million gallons of toxic liquid been drained along a ditch dug with a backhoe right into the creek. When the EPA started to inspect the abandoned factory the agency found forty-eight tons of abandoned super phosphate fertilizer. The walls were saturated with it. "Tim McVee blew up the federal building in Oklahoma City with two tons," Mitchell had said, explaining how volatile the whole situation was. There was a homeless man living in the plant and burning scrap wood for fire. Arkwright was a time-bomb waiting to blow. Also, the whole site was overrun with rats and the snakes that eat them. "You could have filmed *Anaconda* in that old factory," Harold said. Once the EPA got involved in the inspection that would lead to the Arkwright site gaining Superfund designation, the feds kicked state agency DHEC off-site, the first time that had ever happened in South Carolina.

The discovery of the Arkwright dump, located by the EPA while the inspectors were on-site to deal with the IMC assessment, was the second point on Mitchell's "Devil's Triangle." The dump had operated from 1958, when the city incinerator closed, until 1972, when a new city dump opened. It was a thirty-acre landfill that DHEC didn't have records for, though it was on the city's land. "They dug a two hundred foot hole and filled it up—everything—trash, bulk oil, medical waste," Mitchell had explained.

The site was not fenced, and excavations and EPA depositions from the neighborhood show that the local hospital was dumping there, along with much of the industry in the area.

In 1998, the Arkwright community addressed the landfill with the Spartanburg City Council. At the first meeting one-hundred-twenty people showed up in council chambers. There were people there from three communities surrounding Arkwright—lower-income black families, lower-income white families, and middle-income black families.

The third point of the Devil's Triangle was the old Arkwright mill site where we had launched our boats, and where contaminants exist as well: old leaking petroleum tanks. In 1999, the EPA designated the fertilizer plant/dump/ Arkwright mill site part of the Superfund program, and Spartanburg officially had its own little Love Canal. IMC bought the site back that year and put a tent over the plant property, installed monitoring wells, and began the costly, complex clean-up.

When it was clear how extensive the problems in Arkwright were, the neighbors decided to organize the whole lower Southside area and create a "regenesis." The name has a religious ring to it, and soon events took on revival proportions. Six hundred people were at the first organizational meeting to discuss the rebuilding and revitalization of the neighborhoods—black, white, poor, and middle class. The EPA held workshops to address clean-up, educating the community concerning its plight. Soon the number of community members signing on to the ReGenesis vision grew to fourteen hundred.

In the past five years, ReGenesis has grown into a community revitalization organization with 124 partners—public, private, government, non-profits. About $134 million has come into the venture to date. Out of the ReGenesis has grown the model that is being repeated all over the country at similar brownfield and Superfund sites. The ReGenesis model addresses environmental questions, pollution and blight, crime, housing issues, healthcare issues. Why has Harold followed through now for almost ten years? What drove him through all this? "The voices of the dead tend to ring loud in my mind as I press forward," he said in his acceptance speech after winning the Leadership for a Changing World award in 2005.

It's after noon now, and we're strung out along a quarter-mile of shallow water, all paddling in our three separate boats, setting our own pace. Phillip leads the way, his youthful spirit of adventure pushing him downstream in front of the old farts. I'm next. As I float down Fairforest Creek, I keep watching the western shore, looking for signs of the mysterious city dump the EPA discovered in Arkwright's back reaches. I know it's somewhere in the woods. I don't want to paddle past a Superfund site and not see it. But all I see is trees.

"Look, the whole creek's a landfill," GR says, pointing in his canoe. All the way downstream, he's been picking up the brightly colored bottoms of a hundred broken bottles. He'd found them washed up on sandbars and collected them as we passed, a prospector for beauty along the creek's sandy bottom. When I ask him what he plans to do with the bounty of glass, he doesn't know.

"It looks like somebody threw every plastic bag in Spartanburg County in this creek," Gerald says, catching up, pointing to the high water line in the river birches fifteen feet above us.

"They look like prayer flags when the wind blows a little," GR says, paddling his old black canoe forward toward more broken bottles.

I look downstream. There's beauty to be seen in the garbage, though even here a mile or so below the old mill site and the crumbling dam, the creek valley is not a wilderness. It's not *Little House on the Prairie* rural either. There's no patchwork of farm fields and sleepy homesteads with wood smoke drifting from the chimneys. It's nothing but a flat expanse of creek bottom, just like a hundred others, grown up for forty years in privit, kudzu, and spindly hardwoods. It's not even desirable real estate down here. There's no developer out there—except Harold Mitchell—who looks at this flood plain and thinks golf course or anything else. "What would all this mean to a developer?" I ask Gerald as we rest on a sandbar. "Do the developers worry over the idea of development the way we worry over wilderness?"

"I don't think developers sit around and think about what anything means," Gerald says. "They don't do self-critiques or soul-searching when it comes to buying property. They run the numbers. I don't think Roderick Nash has to worry much about his intellectual market share for *Wilderness and the American Mind*. You won't see a book anytime soon called *Development and the American Mind*."

We've had enough talking and we get back in the boats. Our trip is drawing to a close. I can hear the 295 bypass a few hundred yards downstream. Gerald quickly falls a little behind, birding along an opening in the power line that follows the creek all the way, hoping to prolong his day on the creek as long as possible. So what has ReGenesis not addressed so far in its remarkable community revitalization?

Though it calls itself an environmental organization, it doesn't seem from the story that ReGenesis has much to do with traditional environmental issues—species diversity, wilderness, habitat destruction. How much discussion goes on among the partners about what's best for the creek, for all the wildlife, great and small? ReGenesis is a powerful people organization with high hopes for cleaning up and revitalizing the community. I can only hope that they see their community as both the human and non-human world.

There's a plan on the books, with national and state money committed, for cutting a road all the way from South Liberty Street to 295-Bypass, crossing the creek somewhere downstream from the dam, "opening up" the entire area for that golf course and a mixed use village along 295. It seems so remarkable to think that the densely wooded dirty reaches we've paddled through for hours could someday look like any new subdivision with a freshly graded avenue through it.

I can see GR has stopped ahead of me at the outlet for a small clear stream feeding Fairforest from the east. I stop too and ask about Phillip. GR says not to worry—Phillip is already ahead of us at the take-out. He's won the race and now he has to wait a few more minutes while the old guys catch up. I get out of my canoe to stretch my legs.

We haven't seen one human track on our paddle, though Gerald points out an interstate highway of deer prints when he lands on the sandbar. "I hope Mr. Mitchell knows this qualifies as a major urban deer sanctuary," he says. "They probably hide in here and go out and eat people's yards in Duncan Park at night."

I'm still concerned with the question of where is the environment in environmental justice? In the "EJ" movement does environmental concern always get relegated to funding people-friendly hiking trails and planning for "green space" as the money rolls in after clean-up? Once when I brought up the need for more passive green space for Spartanburg, a former mayor asked, "But how will we afford to mow it?"

I tell Gerald we should file our own vision for this place we've paddled through. "I'd like to see at least a hundred of acres of this big Fairforest flood plain cleaned up and left wooded," I say. "I'd sure hope they plan to leave at least a 100-foot riparian buffer along the creek."

Will ReGenesis recognize untended land as sensible stewardship? It's possible. Harold Mitchell is a man who has made a career on listening to all comers with good ideas, even ideas from old conservationists like us. One thing about rich developers, it's hard to get in on the ground floor with their plans, but a community consensus builder like Harold Mitchell is different. The motive for ReGenesis was not profit. It was justice. Maybe the redevelopment of the lower South Side will not be profit driven either.

At my feet, the season's last yellow jackets work the sandbar. In a clear, shallow pool I watch a school of tiny fish feeding, the hopeful signs of the creek's health I've been watching for all along the way. There is plenty of life down here a few miles downstream from Arkwright where one small bold creek feeds another. It's mostly small or fragile life though, overlooked or undervalued by those who occasionally take notice.

If Harold Mitchell wins the race for the South Carolina House in November, these creatures will become some of his smallest constituents. Like Mitchell's African-American ancestors only a few generations ago, wild nature lacks a voice, and it often lacks the justice that comes along with counting. Somehow these fish and yellow jackets and turtles and deer survived in spite of what we've done to make life harder for those most vulnerable—dumps, acid factories, raw sewage seeping from outdated pipes, tons of plastic bags hanging from the trees. Nature creates resilient systems, even the systems we humans call class—rich to poor. Relatively rich visitors like us just walk away at the take-out and leave Arkwright and the creek behind. We're just passing through. I lose focus for a moment, think how I can't wait to get home to take a shower. Then I focus again at the new life earning a living at my feet.

III

Where does the spirit live? Inside or outside
Things remembered, made things, things unmade?

—Seamus Heaney,
from "Squarings"

CIRCUMAMBULATION

Circling a sacred object clockwise is considered holy, so I find a couple of extra days after an academic conference in San Jose to head for the California coast to walk around Marin County's Mount Tamalpais. I've wanted to do the pilgrimage for years, both natural and literary, retracing the steps of poets I've admired and studied, Gary Snyder, Philip Whalen, and Allen Ginsberg. I've wanted to retrace the hike they took the first time in October 1965.

Tradition has it that hikers should do the circumambulation in one day—fourteen miles and twenty-five hundred feet of altitude. There are ten "stages" to the hike, each with its own natural shrine, and though I'm not a very good Buddhist, I plan to chant the appropriate prayers at each stop along the trail established by pilgrims past.

My student Thomas Pierce is with me. He's part of a learning community at Wofford College, a new way—at least for us—of organizing this business of teaching and learning. There are almost a dozen people from Wofford at the conference. Involved in the course with me are my biologist colleague Ellen Goldey and our two students, Thomas and Amelia Snyder. We've worked all summer to shape a pair of linked courses in the humanities and biology around the theme of water.

I believe in the power of "LCs," as we call them, but at times I lose faith entirely in the profession of teaching, especially summers when I'm away from it. Most semesters when I get tired of grading papers, I often ask, "What am I doing? Get to work, experiencing the natural world and writing about it."

Losing faith in teaching is my own failure, born of a sort of unquenchable longing for meaningful writerly work I've never really fully achieved. Writing is lonely and difficult, and it seems to never leave me completely fulfilled. "The real work," Gary Snyder reminds me, when I read him, is often this difficult work—the way raising food or children is difficult, or maintaining community in whatever way we can. Each summer when I sit down at the desk and disappear into essays, poems, and stories, I feel plain besotted with words and sentences for a month or so. Then writing begins to feel like work and the spell wears off, and I long for the consistency and extraverted pleasure of talking with students and teaching classes again. So nothing is easy, not even maintaining contact with the things you love.

Part of the difficulty is that I've chosen as a writer to pursue the lofty goal Faulkner articulated in his Nobel speech—that great writing should be about "the human heart in conflict with itself." I put most of my effort into the clash between the values that shape the human world and that which philosopher David Abram, in his book *The Spell of the Sensuous*, calls "the more-than-human world."

My most fulfilling teaching comes often in the field not the classroom, and my best students over the years have been those who have traveled with me "into the wild." It would be so easy if I could divide my work clearly between the semesters teaching the environmental literature that I love and the summers trying to write such illuminating texts myself. But I'm not that organized. By the time the semester's over I'm often deep in a stupor.

At those times in full summer when writing fails me, even grading papers is better than the difficulty of pushing words up and down a blank page. To keep myself interested in teaching, I've learned to break up my writing time with travel when I'm off and to play pedagogical tricks on myself when I'm not. The latest travel is this trip to California, and the latest trick is learning communities. In a learning community, there's a ready-made audience of learners and colleagues all counting on each other. Teaching in partnership with another professor helps me stay committed to teaching for the duration.

At Wofford College as part of the LC experiment, we offer entering freshmen two linked courses. Ellen's biology course focuses on water and ecology, and my humanities course is shaped around similar themes. We've developed a reading list with both humanities and biology material common to each course—poems, stories, essays, songs, novels in which water appears as an important theme or image. There are also chapters from textbooks about wetlands, streams, and marshes. On Tuesdays we go to class, but Thursdays we've got them all day for long "field experiences." One of my colleagues in the English department was resistant to the idea of humanities students taking part in "field experiences." He could not imagine anything of consequence happening without a blackboard being at the center of it. We call the undergraduates working with us "preceptors" to separate their work from that of lab assistants and give them more responsibility than they would ever likely see as students.

Thomas and I presented a description of our learning community with Ellen and Amelia at the San Jose conference, but we left soon after, professor and preceptor, bent now on a mountain pilgrimage to the wild. Thomas, a sophomore, a lover of the mountains, and a student of fiction, music, and drama, is one of those kids who grows up in a conservative Southern town with a sense that he was born in the wrong place at the wrong time, a sort of reverse Dorothy who wants to kick his heels and chant, "Where else is there?" instead of "There's no place like home." He wears an old brown suede jacket with wide lapels, something you might see Bob Dylan wearing on a 1960s album cover. His hair's a little Dylan-like as well—unruly and two inches too long for the current clipped conservative college look. But Thomas's rebel mold breaks with his perceptiveness, sensitivity, and high standards for his schoolwork, something I was never able to do. He's close to the top GPA among our high achievers. I see this as a good set of signs that the circumambulation of Mount Tamalpias might take with Thomas.

When we leave San Jose, we drive over the mountains toward San Francisco, down Boulder Creek, and stop in the Big Basin State Park full of redwoods. We wander among the giant trees, and I think about how this ecosystem of redwoods used to cover much of the coastal mountains of northern California until all but a remnant was cleared and sold as lumber in the twentieth century. We pass through the stand of old-growth redwoods, and I wonder how much of the large profit from these logging operations went to endow the great universities of the San Francisco Bay area. Was there redwood profit in the salaries of the Nobel laureates? Did the destruction of this vast wild ecosystem fund some of the great thinking of all time? If so, was it a fair trade-off, nature for culture? Would I trade all the advancements in medicine, law, and science that the cutting of these trees probably funded for functioning coastal groves again?

As I brood among the redwoods, Thomas writes fragments he's memorized from the poetry of Theodore Roethke on deciduous leaves with a felt tip pen and drops them along the trail for others to find—"to fall away is always," and "Being myself I sing." Is it littering, he asks, to write lines of poetry on leaves and add them back to the world's compost heap?

Brother Guido Sarduchi on *Saturday Night Live* had a skit called "Five Minute College." He claimed, for a modest fee, he could teach you in five minutes all you'd remember after twenty years from four full years of an undergraduate education. I had five teachers in college I remember with some fondness—two English professors, a philosopher, a geologist, and a sociologist-turned-history professor. The English professors taught me to write and read, the philosopher to think, and the geologist to see, and Ab Abercrombie, the sociologist turned historian, taught me about adventure in the field. I remember little of the information that these teachers shoveled out in class. Only a few of the facts that educators sometimes mistakenly confuse with learning are still available to me now almost thirty years after I earned my undergraduate degree. Instead, my memories of good education are more about moments, about the strong personalities of these five men, about the sudden changes of direction my life took in those formative years.

When I came to college, I thought I wanted to be a high-school basketball coach and teach high-school history in my hometown. By the time I left, I wanted to be Ezra Pound or Loren Eisley. I became neither, but I could not have developed those aspirations without classes in creative writing, Joyce, Pound, and Eliot, existentialism, and historical geology. These teachers were important to me but not as important as Ab. He taught me several classes, but he often took me into the field to "look for critters," which at that time was his passionate avocation. Because of Ab much of my unofficial "general education" was that of wonder. He quickly saw I had an aptitude for curiosity, and to this day that aptitude has led to trips like this one to Northern California. Here among the redwoods I'm carrying on Ab's mission.

Thomas has had me as a professor in two classes, but I don't think it's any "content" I've delivered that has placed him here on the rim of the continent writing poems on leaves. It's an attitude that I hope I'm still modeling. "Get moving and stay moving," my geology professor once said to me. It's good advice for a lifetime, and it made exiting the conference and leaving our colleagues after our obligations were behind us quite easy.

Mid-afternoon Thomas and I are sitting at a ferry dock in the town of Tiburon waiting on the twenty-minute ride over to

Angel Island where we'll backpack in to a remote campsite for a night before coming back to the mainland again for our Tamalpais circumambulation. As we leave the dock there's a sailing camp on the bay. The water is topaz with the looming island behind the sailboats in the distance. One other couple is on the ferry, a man and wife from Arizona car-camping all the way down the California coast. There are three million people in the Bay Area, but tonight it looks like we'll have most of the island to ourselves.

Once on Angel Island, it's a two-and-a-half-mile hike to the campsite. A half-mile up the shady gravel road, we pass old buildings used as a detention center for Chinese immigrants who were held here a year until they were approved for entry or deported. We go inside. A plaque in English explains that there are poems written in Chinese by the immigrants on all the walls. We put down our heavy packs and walk through the empty barracks. The poems are haunting, strings of thin characters flowing down the walls. It's as if the sadness and uncertainty of the immigrants still stain the building's interior. Thomas tries to recreate some of the Chinese characters in his journal. He works at the script with his ballpoint pen. What he comes up with looks like the tracks of gulls on the beach at Tiburon.

I think of Thomas earlier among the redwoods copying out Roethke poems and his deep youthful belief in poetry, its ability to change him. I've lost some of that steady belief now, and it makes me sad for a moment to think how clear poetry's importance is from these leftover stains of occupation. Poetry mattered to these immigrants. Maybe it kept them alive. Though I can't read the Chinese characters, I follow their flow anyway. Are the lines read left to right or right to left? After a few minutes of silent meditation on the poetry, we slip our packs back on and head back out to the road.

As we walk, I begin to ponder the traditional professor-in-front-students-taking-notes classroom teaching model—

what the LC people at the conference derisively call "the sage on the stage." Do I really want to do that for the rest of my life? What did I learn of consequence from the parade of sages on their stages that lectured me through 124 hours of college credit? What do I give my students of consequence during the semesters when I take this approach out of habit and ease? Mostly I teach four or five introductions to literature—general education, they're called. These "service courses" are spiced up with one upper-level creative writing or literature class each semester. Once or twice I've taught environmental literature. The freshman humanities class for which Thomas is preceptor fits into general education, but strangely enough it's become the exception to my early autumn gloom and every year I look forward to the challenge it offers.

In the water class, I'm forced to be the sage up to my knees in creek water with a kick net in my hand, the sage in the raft or canoe, the sage in the back of the room listening to a biology lecture that's over my head, the sage driving the van back from two days at the ocean. In the biology class, I'm the perpetual beginner, circling out into the unknown and leaving any expert's status behind. The change of position is a good thing, no matter whether my stuffy colleague in the tweed coat believes there's any learning of consequence that can take place outside of a dusty classroom with a Ph.D. droning on at the front.

Hiking on Angel Island we encounter a significant uphill, gaining four hundred or five hundred feet of altitude before we finally top out at the remote site we've reserved online. When we arrive at our campsite, there are two German tourists set up in our spot, spread out, obviously hoping that no one would claim the view lot. They sit gazing at the view, drinking wine. We greet them, and they know it's time to pack up and move back into the scrub oak they've been assigned and give up on the better real estate.

We set up our two tiny backpacking tents with the doors opening toward the San Francisco Bay. Across the water, Oakland spreads out to our east, and if we stand on the picnic table, we see the strange tall triangular tower in downtown San Francisco. It's a perfect place to reflect on what Gary Snyder in particular finds compelling about the Bay Area. Wild and urban are always only a few miles apart. Here on this vast natural stage of hills and water and sky, it's possible to believe the two worlds can coexist, Abram's "more-than-human" and the merely human of skyscrapers and jets landing at San Francisco International, less than ten miles apart.

I'm sure Thomas senses all this, but instead of thinking about it all, he spends twenty minutes building a small chain of stones he names "the City Lights snake" between our tents and the island's cliffs. I sling our food from a rope on a nearby tree, spread out our cooking gear—tiny gas stove, plates, gas bottle—on the picnic table, and we set out for the top of Angel Island to see the sun set.

When we return from the summit, it's already dark. My headlamp leading us into camp shows that the cooking gear is nowhere to be seen, and the table is cleared. I scan the scrub oak interior, and the reflections of a dozen raccoons are cast back toward us. The more-than-human world has stripped us clean. We laugh about it and begin to figure out how we'll recover what we need to cook our supper.

Next morning we stop on the way to the Mount Tamalpais trailhead at a Quick Shop for working-class coffee. One guy in overalls says to another buying a honey bun, "Sustenance? What are you doing using those big words?" As I pay for coffee I think, "America, I can almost love you," as Gary said in a poem four decades ago.

Circumambulation. Words don't get much bigger than that. I repeat it to myself as we drive toward Tamalpais. It feels like a quiet chant, and it calms me. I'm a lapsed Methodist, and

Thomas a lapsed Episcopalian, but we both plan to be Buddhists for the day. That's why I'm listening to everything—traffic passing on the early morning freeway, conversation among carpenters in the store—and am headed out to circle Tamalpais. It seems the perfect religious passage for two Southern boys on the West Coast, this age-old mountain pilgrimage. Add to that contact on a good hiking trail with what David Robertson calls "real matter," and I've planned a good outing to forestall the collapse into meaninglessness and to clean out my teaching demons.

Ab taught me in what way travel to wild places can bring you back from the edge of collapse. Four Decembers in a row, in college and afterward, Ab, my friend David Scott, and I would leave Spartanburg and drive to the Everglades in South Florida non-stop, sleep a few hours in our car and hike twelve miles out and back along a canal toward the heart of the park—the vast, distant sawgrass flats and hardwood hammocks on the horizon. On our first trip Ab was transformed from teacher to mentor in escape and wonder. What drew us to the Everglades was catching snakes and spotting birds and the secret hope that we would be in the right place at the right time and see one of the last of the South Florida panthers crossing the trail. As I wheeled the rental car into annex parking at Muir Woods, I realized I was doing the same thing with Thomas thirty years later, as Snyder says at the end of "Ax Handles:" "...model / And tool, craft of culture, / How we go on." I am mentor for adventure this day. We are off into the thick of it with no textbook, no class outside of this mountain.

We start our hike on the Dipsea Trail under the great bay tree in the Muir overflow parking lot where poets Snyder, Whalen, and Ginsberg began their hike as well. At 8:30 A.M. we're off. In our packs: gorp, four Power Bars, two apples, two quarts of water in Nalgene bottles, a bag of peanut M&Ms. We have David Robertson's book *Real Matter* with us to light the way, our only map Robertson's sketch of the pilgrimage route around Mount Tamalpais in his chapter called "Coming Round the Mountain."

I try the trail's early morning coolness with an expedition weight T-neck top but quickly strip down as the heat rises. My shins are sore from hiking on Angel Island. I want to see today, to feel. Oh, mountain, open up to us as we climb and circle your holy summit! We chant Gary Snyder's translation of Buddhism's four vows before we start out: "Beings are numberless: I vow to enlighten them. Obstacles are countless: I vow to cut them down. Dharma Gates are limitless: I vow to master them. The Buddha-Way is endless: I vow to follow through."

In my journal I write, "Cross the little plank bridge and Redwood Creek below. Further on, mixed oak and conifer, little piles of white powder in trail along the way. The oaks in California are dying from a fungus called sudden oak death disease, so Thomas wonders if this powder is some sort of spell against the disease. Jeep trail. Quail and fence lizards along the way. Climbing all the way and the ocean in view to our north. Stopped for water in a redwood grove. Recent fire?"

I used to lean on poetry the way I'm now leaning on a makeshift walking stick I picked up by the side of the trail. When I was young as Thomas, poetry was for me a trail through the deep woods, a secret cave, a waterfall seen from the bottom, the ocean spotted from a distance. Those long ago Decembers as I hiked into the Everglades with Ab and David, I was looking, like they were, for snakes and birds, but I was also looking for ways to bring those creatures back in a web of my own charged language. I felt, like the Chinese immigrants held hostage on Angel Island, that poems could somehow see me through, save me, if I somehow got them out of me and into the world.

Thomas carries with him a collection of Theodore Roethke's poetry journals called *Straw for the Fire*. They are not Roethke's finished poems. Instead they are daily luminescence, the lines the poet scratched in a journal from 1943 to 1963. When we stop, Thomas peels small scraps of Roethke's verse from the book and leaves them drifting through the dry California air. "I'm surrounded by the lint from an enormous navel," he reads matter-of-factly. Or later, as we stop again for water, "So much of experience just flows over me—I might as well be a stone at the bottom of a stream: any stone."

For the moment, Thomas has stopped writing fragments of Roethke's published poetry on leaves and casting them to the fate of others to pick up. Instead he pulls out the book and launches the journal poems into the middle of our circumambulation. These raw passages bring poetry back to me, though I translate the feeling quickly into prose, what I'm most interested in right now. I look around and take notes for what will be an essay: "Ancient interior oak splitting rock outcrop." I look out to see that the ocean is there beyond us to the north, Mount Tam through pines to our east. I work at staying oriented as we circle the mountain.

The wind here is poetry though and will not leave me alone, two pitches, one high and lonesome, the other, closer by. There are lovely views here between stages one and two. Gary, Phillip, and Allen stopped and consecrated this place as sacred in 1965. It's hot up here in holy space. It's still early morning and record heat rising. We're uncertain where Dipsea Trail goes from here. Next stop, Cardiac Hill.

An hour or so later, we've lost the trail but found a California State Ranger instead. He tells us how to find the rest of our route—the Old Mine trail to the rock amphitheater. He says things are very different "here on the north side of the mountain" than where we started our hike "in the rain shadow, more like the Rockies or the High Sierra." We're making good time—a glance at the ranger's watch shows 10:15. He says he knows that trail signs are confusing — "like highway exit signs" showing the way to exit the trail, not what trail you're on. Then the ranger laughs about the administration nightmare to plant new trail signs in California—"Two inches of paper work—state archeologists worried about punching through an Indian skull." We stop at restrooms on the edge of the campground for more water. "If you guys were from Vermont, I'd apologize for the cold today," he jokes, as we head for where he says the trail snakes over the hillside.

In the Rock Springs parking lot, there are crows jabbering in the distance and as we cross a paved road, a lone biker passes us in silence. *Real Matter.* This is it—the ache of miles on my knees, the crows checking us out. The map tells us next stop is Rifle Camp. It's here I wish I knew a little more history of the place, understood why they call it Rifle Camp. As we walk, I think about how foreign the California coast is for me. Dry soil and this strange juxtaposition of blue ocean and bronze mountains. Only the crows stitch it all together with their bickering voices.

Those college trips with Ab taught me how to pay attention, and I try to practice what I learned years ago as Thomas and I climb along the steep dry hillside on Tamalpais's north slope. It's mid-morning and only half as hot as it will be. There are fence lizards and sparrows in the dry grass, common creatures for company.

We can't find station four, Rifle Camp. We've somehow lost the trail, so we stop to eat lunch at Potero Picnic Area. We talk over what happened and Thomas thinks we went wrong when we turned off a trail called Beinstein and followed a sign saying "Rifle Camp" pointed in the opposite direction through a meadow. We followed that meadow trail and found a gravel road but no Rifle Camp. I sit and drink water and eat gorp. Thomas is off exploring our options. We've made good time so far. The summit is next.

I can't ever remember being truly lost on a hike. For me, it happens more often in a canoe. Years ago I was lost in mangrove marsh. The Spanish name of the marsh translated into English is "You'll never get out." Ab and another crocodile biologist were elsewhere in the marsh in a motorboat, and I was in the canoe with two of Ab's students. I was paddling in the canoe's stern, steering us up one blind hall of mangroves after another. We were supposed to be looking for crocodiles, but instead we were looking for a way out. We kept at it until dawn. When we finally worked our way back to a place we recognized we found Ab and his biologist friend sitting silently in the motorboat waiting. He said he was never worried. "We could have found you eventually with an airplane."

Buddha nature is all about paying attention and somehow we miss station five as well. We find a serpentine outcrop that looks suspiciously like the one described in Dave Robertson's book. At station six we chant the four vows next to Collier Springs on a Boy Scout bench among some good tall redwoods. Honeybees dip to the surface of the slight flow in the spring run—dozens of them. This is the only water for some distance around. Is this dry wood what the Southeast will feel like if climate change continues, where water is always at a premium? I look around and compare this landscape with the Blue Ridge Mountains back home we both know so well. I think of a few lines of poetry from Charles Wright, "Landscape's a level of transcendence— / jack-wedge it here,/ Or here, and step back." I'm tired enough so that the transcendence part is easy. I squint, and I can almost see the tiny waterfalls of the Blue Ridge all around me, the deep green shade.

We make an altar out of a redwood stump. I leave a little gorp for these gods and tourist hikers. Thomas leaves a leaf with another Roethke quote along the outer edge of a flat yellow leaf thin as rice paper—"I wake to sleep and take my waking slow."

Inspiration Point has views north and east all the way to Napa Valley. The summit of Mt. Tam is behind us. We have only eight hundred hard feet to go to reach it. That's our goal. It's beautiful on this north side. There are oak woods and chaparral. We saw a deer in the woods just past the point.

Is a hike like this up a mountain a pedagogy of sorts? Is that why some religions like Buddhism place such importance on doing these walks? Is it teaching if the inspiration flows both ways? Who is the master and who is the student? Mountains are often given significance as metaphors for success. Is the summit what it's really about when the valleys and dry ridges offer their own set of lesson plans?

I don't ask Thomas any of these questions as we walk. I simply put one foot in front of another, even though it is getting more and more difficult. Dehydration is setting in. I've consumed four or five quarts of water, but I'm dry as the trailside. In some ways, I've thought of this hike as a sort of test before I turn fifty in two years. Right now I can't tell if I've passed the test or failed. At least the mythic summit is in sight. I can't see how we could possibly lose our way from here.

"I believe in a non-state governed by Rites and music," Snyder once said, explaining his political position as an anarchist. We're doing our part today, trying to play out this rite of passage, this long strange day trip. We've already missed two of the seven stages though. Is a rite still a rite if you do it wrong? My brain is drying out, and I turn this question into a mantra as we inch up toward the summit.

In *Real Matter*, David Robertson says rite and ritual allow "human beings to negotiate with presences beyond the human." We've seen those presences as we've inched up the mountain—rock, trees, insects, lizards, hawks and vultures, deer in the shadows. Snyder, Whalen, and Ginsberg all wanted, with their hike, to "open a door through which future generations could continually enter the mountain." And now in a trick of sunlight as Thomas walks the trail in front of me, I see his body walk slowly through the mountain, and I follow.

We're on the summit. It's twenty-five hundred feet in the air, the whole bay is below us. I sit and drink another quart of water, my bottle filled in the bathroom at the road's end. We didn't see another hiker the whole way around and now here on the summit there are several groups of tourists. They've driven up and now walk the last three hundred yards up to Gardner Lookout with us. There are Monarchs here at the top, flitting around. We can see Angel Island is in the distance. How much lower were we on Mt. Livermore? I don't think I've ever been as hot as I am now. I need to drink water and rest for a minute.

From the summit down, it's all survival, and a combination of the unseasonable heat and our lack of a map has made the end of the hike difficult. We take Fern Canyon Trail, which empties eight hundred feet down the mountain on a gravel road, then we continue to the Old Stage Coach Inn where we get a drink of water. There we turn right instead of a left and end up missing the last station (Mountain Home) and so don't go down the Ocean View Trail. We use Bootjack Trail instead through the redwoods leading down into Muir Woods proper.

As we approach the grove, the steep dirt single-track gives way to the tourist-friendly asphalt ribbon that is the Hillside Trail, an outing millions have taken through the tourists' woods. By this time I am almost delirious with thirst. The trees get bigger and bigger as do the crowds the closer we get to the Visitor's Center. I'm dreaming of Mexican food in Mill Valley, of lemonade, of sticking my head under the faucet in the bathroom, of bringing this pilgrimage to a close.

I'm leading as we walk though the tourist weirdness of Muir Woods. I pass men, women, and children of many colors and sizes, some dressed in the brightly colored costumes of their cultures. The children try to duck the railing to play in the creek. The adults all look up, their necks set to acquire cricks. Though I'm fascinated by the sociology experiment underway in the tourist woods, I'm on a forced march to find relief from my fatigue and dehydration. After ten hours on the trail, I'm a medical emergency waiting to happen. My knees grate as they swing my legs reluctantly down the trail. My tee shirt is stiff and clotted with more (sweat) salt than the Dead Sea.

I stop to sit on a bench next to one of the tourist trees named after an American president. I'll wait here for Thomas who is taking his time behind me on the trail. I need to take this in before we pass on through to overflow parking. Muir Woods is possibly the greatest shrine to what I want to witness to in the world—the more-than-human one-thousand-year-old redwoods standing before me, admired, even worshipped in a culture that almost always values 2x4s more than old growth.

Thomas shows up and looks up at the redwood, then glances around at the tourists looking up as well. He offers no Roethke poetry. "Weird scene" is all he says as commentary. He's looking really no worse for the wear of the day. He's thirty years younger and in much better hiking shape. For some reason, I think of a moment when we first arrived in California. I'm with the whole Wofford group and the conference hasn't started. There are seven or eight of us in two rental cars. We have driven north on the Coast Highway to see a lighthouse on a lonely stretch above Monterrey. In the car with me was a smart but narrow undergraduate pre-med major acting as a preceptor for another class. All the way up the glorious coast the pre-med student talked on his cell phone to a girlfriend 3,000 miles away. He didn't see a thing, caught like a fly in the web of his own heart—a heart not in conflict. The day before we'd talked about some sort of environmental literacy class being a requirement for an undergraduate degree, and this student had argued that material had little to do with his success or failure in his future as a doctor and he'd resent such a requirement.

What would that young man see here? I don't ask Thomas. I don't want to sound like a condescending adult educator disappointed at the shallowness of today's students. But I would like to know if that pre-med student so juiced on his own future as a doctor would see what we see among these ancient big trees. "Let's get moving," I say to Thomas and stand up slowly in the light falling from high up in the redwoods.

Thomas heads on down the trail, and when I follow, the student becomes the teacher and the teacher the student who learns by hiking. It's now less than a quarter-mile back to the rental car, and I'm not prepared to do any more thinking. Circling this mountain has worn me out. There was a great Larson cartoon years ago. It showed five or six big lugs sitting in a classroom. One raises his hand and asks the professor, "Could I be excused? My head is full."

CARNIVAL AGAINST CAPITALISM

Rouse up, O Young Men of the New Age! Set your foreheads
against the ignorant Hirelings! For we have Hirelings in the Camp,
the Court & the University, who would, if they could, for ever
depress Mental & prolong Corporeal War.
—William Blake, from his preface to *Milton*

Back in June 1999, my family and I were looking for something
to do in London on a Friday night. We had just finished dinner
at Wagamama's, a noodle bar near the British Museum. I
thought the boys would like those strange Monty Python look-
alike commercials that run at the beginning of movies in the
United Kingdom, so Betsy picked up a copy of *The Daily
Telegraph* at a nearby newsstand. Searching for the entertain-
ment section she made an offhanded comment: "John, this
sounds like your kind of demonstration." She showed me the
tiny notice in the paper announcing that ten thousand were
expected for "The Carnival against Capitalism" in London that
day. We both laughed, mentioned my anti-Wal-Mart
journalism back home and my fight against the development
of a local Girl Scout camp. I laughed too, then suggested we
instead spend a quiet evening in Trafalgar Square so the boys
could feed the pigeons some seeds laced with birth control.

When we exited the tube at Leicester Square there were
more strange Londoners than usual, even for a Friday night. A
man in a hurry to get somewhere pushed us aside as we hit the
street. He had a Mohawk made of Barbie legs, and he was
wearing a dress. We followed him out into what quickly
proved to be the "carnival" the paper had warned was likely.
Leicester Square was crammed. After a brief walk we saw that
Trafalgar Square was swarming with thousands of revelers,

and hundreds of riot police formed semicircles around both ends of the park.

I'm telling you what I saw on that long-ago summer vacation because you will not have read about it in any major US publication. That day tens of thousands worldwide were making their stand against what they saw as the dark side of capitalism, and the world media chose to ignore it. That makes it news. The riot police had on black helmets with face masks and carried rounded clear shields like high-tech Roman warriors. A black police helicopter hovered directly over the National Portrait Gallery, and small pods of Asian tourists hugged the steps of Saint Martin in the Fields, one of Christopher Wren's original churches. They pointed their long lenses into the frolicking protesters. There wasn't a pigeon for blocks.

Hundreds of protesters were using the huge lions around Lord Nelson's statue for a jungle gym. Someone had spraypainted "Pigs Are Scum" on the statue's base, and semi-nude men and women in tie-dyes swam like porpoises in the two biggest basins of the huge fountain. Everyone was laughing (except the police), and there was a sense of merriment in the air, Robin Hood come to the city.

I have told this story many times since returning to the States, and I always call the crowd in the park "hippies," but that is an anachronism from over thirty years in the past. What were they, I wondered as I looked down into their midst? Counter-culture? Underclass? Dispossessed Post-Thatcher Youth? Rob and Russell, aged twelve and nine, were born long after the 60s had settled down, and they were not splitting such hairs. "This is really fun," they said. "More fun than the torture museum?" I asked. More fun than the tube, the double-decker buses, and the Tower of London combined, they surmised. The boys were caught up in the intense color and energy of it all. One picture we took shows Russell with a purple-headed woman squeezed in close beside him. The boys were transfixed and seemed fearless. They had less experience with riot police and carnivals than I did, but they were like heat-seeking missiles to the blaze of the crowd.

They pulled their two older, more cautious guardians to the concrete rail encircling the park. Below us were young men and women in various stages of dress, with blue and purple hair, with dreadlocks and Mohawks, playing Frisbee with dogs and hacky sack with friends. It was Woodstock with an accent and no music. The Crosby, Stills, Nash, and Young song "Chicago" kept racing through my head. Had we somehow wandered into history? Yes, we worried about the riot police. Yes, we worried when a girl walked up and whispered, "They killed a girl earlier today, the police. They ran over her with a van." We were the responsible ones, the guardians. But what's safer, a life of well-beaten tourist tracks and double-decker tour buses, or a once-in-a-lifetime opportunity to see, as Buffalo Springfield put it, "...something happening here, what it is ain't exactly clear." This was better than a movie, but we all agreed sensibly we'd move across the street with the Asian tourists on the steps of the old church if the police surged from their cautious semicircles on each end of the park.

We stood for an hour at the railing. The longer we were there I began to sense that the revelers were tired, that the worst of something (just what we would not find out until the next day) had already passed like a dark shadow. This was the end of a long day, not the beginning of a night carnival. Then, behind us on the street, between the park and the church, a number of young men with whistles were stopping the three lanes of traffic circling around Trafalgar Square, and a big-muscled black man rode an old ten-speed through the creeping cars. The police watched, not moving to stop them. We finally moved from the park railing when a large group of the protesters stopped a white stretch limo and started to rock it and taunt the driver. It was a frightening moment as twenty teenagers kicked the car and yelled at the driver and shook the limo back and forth. Around the corner came an image of home: a grey BMW roadster with a big guy driving. One of the protesters dervished over the hood. Another grabbed the guy's Nike hat. Even the boys were a little scared at that point, so we quickly moved to the other side of the street, placing a line of riot police between us and the stalled uncomfortable London traffic. The scene could turn ugly or it could simmer for hours more. After a few more minutes, we headed back to our hotel.

The next day when we left London, I began to understand how significant the event we had witnessed had been. As I scoured the papers for details, I began to think of it as my riot. I was a man possessed with detail. I felt I was finally a part of history, living and breathing. I pulled together what we had seen the night before—after all, we were eyewitnesses to radical history— and added it to the numerous press reports. "Mobs put city under siege," *The Daily Telegraph's* headline exclaimed. "Mayhem" *The Express* added in bold black letters. Mayhem! We had been part of the mayhem!

We had come across the burnt-out end of a world-class protest/riot the 1960s would have been proud to call its own— one of the papers was calling it the worst in the city of London since the poll-tax riots of the early 1990s; another called it the worst trouble in the financial district since the Gordon Riots of 1780. There had been no one killed, though the girl circulating through the crowd was right about one thing: hours before we arrived on the scene the police had run over two people with their vans.

The event, called June 18th or J18, had been organized for over a year, had an extensive web site and it was "timed to coincide with the first day the Group of Seven (or G7) summit of the leaders of the richest nation-states in Koeln, Germany" when again, as the J18 website explains, "we will be told by the economic and political elites that the promotion of economic globalization, 'free' trade and corporate dominance is the only way."

The web site explains J18 as a "day of protest, action and carnival in financial centres across the globe"; as planned it was to be "an international day of action aimed at the heart of the global economy: the financial centres, banking districts and multinational corporate power bases." The protesters would include "environmentalists, workers, the unemployed, indigenous peoples, trade unionists, peasants groups, women's networks, the landless, students, peace activists and many more who are working together in recognition that the global capitalist system, based on the exploitation of people and the planet for the profit of a few, is at the root of our social and ecological troubles." Nowhere did J18 advocate violence. The gatherings, in forty countries around the globe, were to be "demonstrations, actions, protests, pickets, stunts, shut-downs, leafletting, blockades, games, carnivals, sit-downs, free food, occupations, and parties." Ghandi and King would be proud.

During the 1960s the youth had taken over government buildings and college administration buildings; in the late 1990s the target of protest had shifted to stock exchanges, banks, and corporate headquarters.

Saturday morning the financial district in London wore the look of a battle-zone with £2 million worth of damage. Forty people had been taken to the hospital. Fifteen had been arrested. Some of the thousands of protesters had wrecked a McDonalds, broken into a Mercedes showroom, and trashed several cars, forced entry into the Liffe Futures Exchange and the nearby Rabobank.

The encounters between the protesters and financial workers had taken on mythic proportions. When the rioters broke into the London Futures Exchange, traders in three-piece suits had retreated to the upper floors where they taunted the protesters below by waving their gold American Express cards out open windows, chanting "We're rich; you're not. We're rich; you're not." They had even photocopied fifty- and one-hundred-pound notes and showered the unruly crowds with a capitalistic ticker tape.

There were wondrous rumors as well: that rioters had built a wall, blockading the Liffe Futures Exchange, and that one protester had Superglued his head to the door of the Bank of England. Though most news reports suggested that the movement claims no leaders, the names of the organizations involved in the worldwide protest were widely reported: Reclaim the Streets, an anti-car movement that disrupts London's traffic regularly because "the car system steals the street from under us and sells it back for the price of petrol;" Jubilee 2000, a group campaigning for Third World debt to be written off in the new millennium; Critical Mass, a pro-cycling organization that forms large groups and rides through London disrupting traffic; InterContinental Caravan, a group of people traveling through Europe protesting against worldwide economic structures and activities of multinational corporations, and genetically modified foods; and my two favorites, the Association of Autonomous Astronauts, which protests the military use of space; and the Biotic Baking Brigade, which is famous for throwing custard pies at prominent people.

One long editorial by Jonathan Freedland in *The Manchester Guardian* made the best argument for the importance of what had happened in London that first day of our vacation. Freedland's "The Theater of Riot" argues that the rioters could not be dismissed as "masked thugs" or "hate-filled youths" or "evil savages." They were part of the British way of life. The riot in London "may be the latest example of a long British tradition of dissent, one that stretches back to the earliest days of English, Welsh, and Scottish history." Freedland asks, "And what if the sheer similarity of the current 'mob' to rebels past offers a sharp warning to the governing class—in Britain and beyond?"

John Lane

An unsigned editorial in *The London Times* took an opposite position: "And what does the home security think about rioting at the centre of Britain's multi billion-pound international financial district? It was poor advertisement for doing business here." *The Daily Telegraph's* editorial writer suggested, "Bankers, traders and stockbrokers are the real working class."

What to make of it after putting thousands miles of distance between myself and the riots? What fascinates me most is how the protest was not covered in the United States. It happened here as well, so maybe Freedland's warning to the governing class should be taken to heart. There were dozens arrested on Wall Street in a similar "Carnival Against Capitalism," and six hundred protesters formed a human chain around the Treasury building in Washington, much as Vietnam War protesters had circled and tried to levitate the Pentagon in the late 1960s. The US press ignored this worldwide protest. There was nothing in the *New York Times,* nothing in *Newsweek* or *Time.* I guess the royal wedding took up all the space allotted to Great Britain for the week.

I missed the 60s and I've always regretted it. The closest I ever got to the roaring political ferment of Chicago or Haight-Ashbury was a rock festival in Spartanburg's Duncan Park in 1968 (I was fourteen) with ten local bands, blankets, Peter Max bubble lettering, and one or two scrawled references to "pigs" and "peace." I get a faculty friend to repeat the story over and over of several professors and a handful of students leaving the Wofford campus and marching on Spartanburg's city hall—protesting the Vietnam War. Marching on city hall seems so out of character to buttoned-down Upstate South Carolina. But now I can add my story to my old faculty friend's. I too have been on the ragged edge of social change. Maybe it's my childhood, but I've never been deeply repelled by chaos and rebellion on a massive scale. As I stood with Rob, Betsy, and Russell looking into Trafalgar Square, I found myself siding with the carnival more than with the black-suited riot police or the more abstract presence of capitalism. I don't find violence romantic, but I don't find complete control and order much more compelling. I was glad for the boys to see that there are people out there in the world unsettled by issues we mostly perceive as settled law: consumer culture, the hierarchy of traffic flow over people, the comfort of order over chaos. On a personal level, the events of June 18 assured me that we are still a democracy in the making. If there is to be revolution in the future, I feel certain it will come as a result of the widening gap between rich and poor. June 18th in London looked a little like the future could look: the dispossessed pushing into the places of economic power and the powerful taunting them from above. What was it Jefferson said about a little foment?

A Week of Mexican Waterfalls

Just before Christmas of 2003, my family and I are on a bus rolling west across thirty dusty miles of coastal plain between Mexico's Tampico and Cuidad Valles on a straight, flat, pot-holed two-lane highway lined on both sides with sugar cane. The pace of contemporary Mexican bus travel is staccato. We are either barreling along at 100 km or slowed to a near stop behind a donkey cart. The drivers have evolved an intricate system of communication between buses, hand signals that make them look like baseball umpires signing to batters. The Spanish they speak is either a language to stave off disaster or simply amuse each other as they pass.

We four sit across the front of the bus—Betsy and me in one double seat, Rob and Russell in the other. As we roll along, the boys listen to American music on CD players. I daydream how it might have been just like this driving between American cities in the 1930s—but here is modern bus-and-truck traffic mixed in with transportation that goes back to the Spanish conquest.

I've been to Mexico a half a dozen times, mostly on wildlife study working as a research assistant to scientist friends. My visits have often served as a screen on which I project my nostalgia for a better, earlier America, a strange pastime that I am initiating my new family into for the first time on this trip. This is the first time since England we've been on an extended vacation together.

I'll admit I am looking forward to the paddling down a river as well. For fifteen years, my life was centered in rivers. Seasons revolved around water levels and weekend paddling road trips. Most recently I've spent more time writing about rivers than paddling them. Mexico is a chance to get back to "river time" for a week.

Mostly though this trip is about Mexico, the full body immersion of it. I want to put the country back on like a body stocking. The bus ride to Cuidad Valles gives me plenty of time to think about Mexico. Before Cortez arrived, no one in the Western hemisphere had the wheel except for those found on toys, so if there were ancient hand signals on this old Meso-American *Cameno Real* (Royal Road), they were between Native American couriers running up from the coast with fresh seafood for the king. The first conquistadors, led by Cortez, landed south of here in 1518 and marched inland to challenge the Aztec empire. In a few years, he'd conquered the whole country, and what poet William Carlos Williams calls "the Flower World" was gone. The cultural loss was staggering, and only now through archeology and genetics is the story now coming into focus. More and more the scholars are making clear how throughout the hemisphere languages vanished, styles of art, music, and ceramics all disappeared under the onslaught of the European invasion, and what we have now is one consumer culture that has eaten old Tampico since I was last there almost a decade before.

Driving from the airport our first night in Mexico, I note the spread of fast food along the highway into town—Wendy's, Burger King, even a Taco Bell. CNN is available on every TV. Everyone has a cell phone. Having passed through Tampico, I can't wait to get further inland and fool myself into believing everyone in the world is not becoming us. Driving west, I see the mountains in the distance, and I turn and tell the boys that there are rivers blue as swimming pools falling through them that we will paddle. They flip their headphones down for a moment and listen. I am talking about adventure, and that's what we've promised them.

Estimates now say there could have been as many as twenty-five million native people in central Mexico when the Spanish arrived on the coast, and one hundred years later there are only seven-hundred thousand left. It wasn't until 1968 that the modern Mexican population density reached similar percentages again. Mostly the natives were killed off by the invisible invaders from Europe—small pox, measles, plague, hantavirus. Our mission on our Mexican vacation is less dramatic and hopefully not destructive, a week-long foreign beachhead upgraded to the twenty-first century. It is a family vacation right out of *Outside's* list of "100 things you should do before you die"—a week paddling rapids and travertine waterfalls ranging in height from eight feet to over twenty feet on three separate rivers—the Micos, Tiburon, and Salto.

At the bus station in Valles, we were met by Grant Amorial, the tall, rangy American proprietor of Agua Azul Whitewater, a company I'd found with a simple internet search. When we walk into the dusty station someone yells "John," and we turn and Grant is there, sitting on a shoe-shine stand with a cell phone to his ear. "The tall skinny gringo" is how he'd said we'd know him. The shoe shine is perfect. He leans back, and a Mexican boy shines his old boots. The only resident American in Valles, Grant likes to play it up.

Grant stands, shakes hands all around, wearing seventeen years of Mexican whitewater adventure (He pioneered many of these Sierra rivers.) on his tanned, lined face. He seems a little impatient to get out of town, says his Mexican guide Pollo is out looking for us, so Grant hustles us out of the station. When I look at Grant, I am struck right away with how old I have become in the last ten years. Approaching fifty, I'm out of paddling shape. Grant is ten years younger, but his life is still rigged to keep him lean and active. Twenty years ago I believed that I too would end up like Grant, living in a tropical country pushing whitewater adventure on tourists from the north. Instead I became a college professor, writer, and more recently, a father and husband, and now most of my adventure is recreated, like this one, in my head, a Class IV imagination accompanying me to my desk each morning.

Pollo, our young guide and driver soon hustles up, loads us in the big red and black Agua Azul Suburban, a shuttle vehicle he called "Pepe" with a kayak cage on top. Grant says he'll see us at camp and vanishes into Valles to run errands. We roll through the busy streets of the bustling farming city of almost one-hundred thousand packed in between two slow valley rivers with mountains rising to the west. Pepe the Suburban is quite a rig and looks like it has one-hundred thousand Mexican miles on it. Pollo's English is good but broken, and he talks nonstop. He is from a middle-class Mexican family in St. Luis Potsi, east of the mountains. He is a climber, mountain biker, and kayak guide. When I say that Grant seemed upset we were late arriving from Tampico, Pollo laughs and says, deepening his Mexican accent for affect, "Grant? Et ees part of the show, no?"

I laugh too. You can find a thousand young people just like Pollo working the rivers of North Carolina or Colorado, outdoor migrants who follow the tourists from whitewater to snow and back to whitewater again the next year. They are young adventurers, and I know our boys find this attractive. Pollo's part of an industry and a lifestyle only available to the upper classes until well into the twentieth century—outdoor adventure—poorly paid to do what they love with water, wind, or snow. I envy his freedom and youth, but realize I am now one of the tourists he is staging the show for and settle back in the seat for the ride. We are in Mexico, and I will let it wash over me.

We drive out of town, and Pollo stops Pepe on a rise and points out a dramatic gash in the mountain front still ten miles west where the Rio Micos pours out—"the canyon." We drive toward it for fifteen minutes, first on a paved highway lined with sugar cane, and then finally onto a two-track that descends a mile to the river past huts with thatch roofs, pigs, goats, and outdoor cooking sheds. Pollo says Grant's encampment is called "The Ranch," and it is on banks of the

127

Rio Micos, at the mouth of the canyon we could see from outside of Valles.

As we descend to the river, Pollo explains how the ranch was built on top of a Huestec ceremonial site. As we drive in, we see the mounds in the milpas all around. Pollo says the ground is littered with pot shards, bones, and basalt blade fragments, though, of course, we aren't allowed to keep any since this pre-Columbian litter is part of the cultural heritage of Mexico and taken very seriously by the government.

As we unload, Pollo describes with great pride how the Huestecas "kicked Cortez's butt" in 1520 and lived an extra fifty years without Spanish domination. Betsy, Rob, and Russell's faces tell me they know as well that this is a pretty remarkable place. A pyramid mound is next to the cook hut and serves as the site of a red radio tower, and the stones that line the pyramid have become stepping stones, retaining walls, and foundations for Grant's outpost. Adaptive reuse, the archeologists call it. Grant has a ragtag group of locals working for him—Pedro the driver, Pollo the guide, Margarita the cook, and three or four others who work the yard crew, most of them, Pollo explains, paid four or five dollars a day. He says everyone wants to work for Grant because it beats cutting sugar cane.

Soon after we settle in, Pollo gathers gear, and Pedro drives us upstream to the Cascadas de Micos, a section of limestone travertine ledges ("teacup falls," they call them) and slow, deep blue pools—only two miles upstream from the ranch. As we "gear up" on the road above, Pollo explains that we'll walk a hundred stone steps with our boats down the wall of the canyon then paddle back to "the Ranch" for supper—2 miles below. Sugar-cane trucks rattle past; "Rasta trucks," Rob calls them, the cane sticking out from all sides.

We follow Pollo down the long steep stone stairway as Betsy watches. We look like a line of brightly colored beasts with the kayaks balanced on our shoulders. I rest on a small overlook as the boys and Pollo descend, and below I see for the first time the initial waterfall we'll run on the Micos, an eighteen-foot drop into a blue pool. At the water's edge we slip into our boats at the top of the falls and Pollo floats up to the sharp horizon line and drops off backward. Part of the show.

And so we follow Pollo all that first afternoon into adventure—Rob, Russell, then me. What is it like running a waterfall? It's like a parachute jump into a rushing faucet. It is a Tinker Bell flight with a blue pool at the bottom. It is one of the greatest acts of release I've ever experienced—paddle, let go, and whoosh, one second, two seconds, water all around you sparkling, then you're down below, bobbing back to the surface with a smile and some serious perspective on gravity.

Downstream on the Micos, there are ten travertine falls over eight feet before the cascades quiet down in a small regional park and pool where the locals swim. From the park, the last few ledges are amazing to look at—vegetation growing all over them—green ferns, blooming flowers, caves thick with a plant that looked like a philodendron. The Rio Micos is the river Walt Disney would have built. There are spots on the Micos where you can sit in a pool and look back upstream and see three or four travertine falls lined up, a green and blue stairway to a tropical heaven.

That night Russell convinces Grant to drive us all back into Valles to find the Carolina Panthers football game showing somewhere in a bar. We find one place willing to switch from soccer to American football and sit there all night watching the game in Spanish. The game goes into overtime, and we leave before it was decided, much to Russell's frustration.

We sleep that night in thatch huts made of mud and bamboo beside the remarkably blue water of the Rio Micos. The next morning, Pollo asks Betsy if she had heard "the carrots," meaning the green parrots that were flying up and down the river. On our second day, Rob and Russell go with Grant to paddle the Rio Salto with more waterfalls, including one twenty-three feet high. Betsy and I drive with Pollo two hours deeper into the mountains to see the "eccentric gardens" of Edward James in the little mountain town of Xhilitla. All the way, Pollo tells us stories about the mountains and talks about the native people who survive there. He has a deep respect for these mountain people. "This is the heart of Mexico," he says with pride as we pass more and more people who are obviously of native descent. He tunes the radio to an indigenous station, and we listen to a scratching fiddle tune that goes on forever, all the way up the mountains. Pollo becomes very excited when the announcer speaks Heusteca: "Listen, no Spanish!"

The garden in Xhilitla, called Los Posos ("The Pools") is inspired by Edward James's friend Salvidor Dali and was built in the 50s and 60s. Pollo hires a guide who arrives on a moped and gives us a good long tour. There are concrete flowers, optical illusions, long stairways that disappear, a wild waterfall and creek, all falling slowly back into the Mexican jungle. Then our guide jumps back on his moped and leads us into the town. It is market day in Xhilitla, and so we wander around and see the sixteenth-century mission church and "the indigenous ones" as Pollo calls them, the ones who come to town and sell their pottery and their tamales.

The next day is a long one on a more traditional drop pool river, much like the Chattooga through a deep canyon—the Rio Tampion. Betsy floats down in raft. I have a bad swim in the worst rapid, but Rob and Russell rescue me just fine. Pollo paddles up beside me, smiling, saying, "Part of the show!"

After the swim the rest of the day has a little edge to it, but it is grand down in that deep Mexican canyon. The river has carved the limestone so it looks like a pipe organ. Where the Rio Tampion empties out of the canyon, it disappears completely underground. This portage, about twenty yards, is called Pueto de Dios, the Bridge of the Gods, and since it is the winter solstice (December 21) Grant explains how the sun will later line up perfectly with a Huesteca ceremonial site to the east and set over the natural bridge. The site is where we will take out and load for the drive home. We will be lined up in our own way with the pre-Colombian past.

The next day, we all go back to the Rio Salto so I can paddle it, and we take Betsy along. The boys run the twenty-three-foot waterfall again, and Betsy and I watch from a downstream eddy where we will join them for the rest of the river. Grant has borrowed a long yellow sit-on-top kayak for Betsy. It looks like she is paddling a banana. We head downstream. In this boat, Grant is able to slip Betsy through the easiest routes, and twice she has to throw her kayak down and then jump fifteen feet or so into a plunge pool below. She runs two waterfalls close to eight feet and somehow stays on her boat. The Salto is a beautiful wild river, with cane, cedar, and of course all those ferns like we've seen on the Micos. My two favorite waterfalls on the trip are on this section—each dropping about fifteen feet into a blue pool.

On the Salto we take out just above a 90-foot falls with our hearts thumping. There are Mexicans watching from the overlook, and two overweight girls get an instant big crush on Rob and won't leave him alone. They hoot and whistle as he takes off his PFD (personal floatation device) and paddling jacket. On the way back, we stop at "tacoria" in a small town and eat a plate of soft tacos—beef, onion, cilantro, and salsa verde washed down with "brown" Coronas, the local beer and Cokes in glass bottles made with real cane sugar.

And so it went. We remained adventure tourists for our first two days in Mexico, suspended outside of the local, but on the way back from the Rio Salto, something changed. The change fell over us all like light or weather. For an hour, we cruised in Pepe the Suburban with our boats on top through endless sugar-cane fields, and they somehow rose in my mind in importance. We hopped from the drainage of the Salto into the upper watershed of the Micos, Grant's "home river." We were an hour above where the clear Micos falls through the cascades of the canyon. It was not only the rivers and the perfect blue waterfalls we were experiencing on this trip. It was those endless fields as well.

On the way back, Grant and the driver discussed which ruined and abandoned power poles along the route they could "salvage" in order to push electricity a mile downhill to the ranch, the next big project for Agua Azul. Grant said we were the probably the last group to experience the ranch "off the grid," a distinction I hold dear. Once we began to talk about electricity, Grant began to tell stories of how it only came to this area in the 1970s and how there are still shop owners who will sell power to many low-wage camposinos who they allow to illegally tap into their line, and how these shop owners will sometimes owe thousands of dollars on bills that go back all the way to the installation of the original lines, and the national electric company will just let them slide. "Coming into the twentieth century hasn't been an easy transition in the countryside," Grant laughed.

Later, at my insistence, Grant gave us all a brief history of the sugar-cane industry. Cane, he explained, is a grass originally from New Guinea but brought to Mexico soon after the conquest. After it's planted it grows back for eleven years. "It's got a six month growing season, then they burn the fields," Grant said. "They burn them at night so that nobody sees the smoke, the visual evidence of the pollution." The burning gets rid of the dry leaves, clears the fields of snakes, and also causes the water to be sucked out of the roots, making the stalks heavier. After the fields are burned only the cane is left, cut by hundreds of hands holding machetes as it's always been. "The burning's called 'cortar,' and the harvest, 'cafra.'"

After burning and harvest, the long-cut cane is loaded on big open-sided trucks and hauled to the refinery. There are seven refineries dotted throughout the region. The cane comes in, is dropped off, chopped again, and boiled down in huge vats. The dirty smoke from the refining fills the upper valley of the Micos. The cane waste is burned to fuel the refining. As we passed the local refinery on the way back from the Salto, we saw the huge smokestacks billowing black smoke, and Grant pointed out a big settling pond out back for water. "At least they have a pond," Grant said, "and don't release it directly to the river."

As we passed through the miles of sugar-cane fields, Grant explained how big changes were underway in the "cane culture," traditions which stretched all the way back to colonial times. There are 10,000 who still follow the way of the cane in the region west of Tampico. An American in the valley has introduced mechanical harvesting—Grant pointed out the trucks with solid sides and how the cane is cut into small pieces by the machines. These were the trucks filled by the mechanical harvesters.

"How will these 10,000 people in the region make what little living they have if not cutting cane?" Betsy asked. "If that work disappears as an economic force, where will they go?"

"They'll probably head for Mexico City to join the other thirty million poor people there. Mexico has one-hundred million people and only five million live above the poverty line. It's hopeless here. No chance to move up, to improve. The elite and middle class are fixed, and at the bottom, the camposino is fixed. If you're born camposino, you die camposino."

"What about the Mexicans working in the north? There are thousands around Spartanburg where we're from," Rob asked.

"It's the only way to move up—to go north. Oil used to be Mexico's number one industry. Now it's money from the north coming back into the country from those working legally and illegally there. It's a complex story you're driving through. It's something not on most of the tourist trails."

The next day, our last, we paddle the Micos again, and Betsy is supposed to meet us at the little public park below the waterfalls and paddle the last mile of river with us back to camp in her yellow sit-on-top. When we arrive at the park, Betsy isn't there, and we head downstream assuming she'd decided not to. After a mile, we see her floating ahead of us on her yellow banana. She turns, thrilled to see us since she'd gotten confused and gone down by herself. She says Pedro, the shuttle driver, spoke no English and so she didn't really know where to wait for us. She's had a solitary adventure running a mile of river alone, and it is the biggest adventure of the trip for her. "All the way down, I kept waiting for the poison darts to come zinging out," she says.

So ended our week of Mexican adventure. The next guests at the ranch would have electricity after Grant and his crew ran grid power down the hill using scavenged power poles. If we ever go back, Russell might not have to drive into town to watch his beloved Panthers play American football in the wilds of Mexico. Eric Leed, in *The Mind of the Traveler*, says the modern tourist often carries a nostalgia for the time "when travel was truly travel, when there were boundaries between the known and unknown, civilized and uncivilized, when escape was still possible."

Escape is not an option any more. The tourist supply routes are easy. The grid is now nearby—phone service, internet, TV, paved roads. Our bus ride back to Tampico is uneventful—from Pepe we load our gear on a first-class bus in Valles complete with American video. It is an American comedy full of cheap jokes and recycled humor. An hour later we are in Tampico, and soon after we were winging our way back toward "El Norte." The boys mostly sleep through their easy transition from Mexico to Texas to South Carolina. Do they now dream of Mexico, of waterfalls and breaking the surfaces of a hundred blue pools in a week? Or do they dream of fields of cane?

THE SHAPE OF ONE JOURNEY

I.

In the Lima airport the light is bright but lifeless. My transcontinental flight landed well after midnight, and the last leg of the trip, a brief hop inland to Cuzco, is not until mid-morning. I spent the night sleeping on the cool terminal floor rather than sort through hundreds of Peruvians screaming "taxi" and "hotel" outside the arrival gates of the terminal. To depart with one of these strangers would mean I'd end up somewhere out in the vast dark reaches of this South American coastal city. I realize I'm not off to a very adventurous start—paralyzed by fear in the Lima airport, afraid to venture out and get a cab, secure a hotel. What's the worst that could have happened to me? Overcharged by the cabbie? Instead I opt for wandering like an inmate in the concourses lined with signs for a local soft drink called Inka Kola.

Around me in the food court are a handful of choices for staying awake: Dunkin' Donuts, Papa John's familiar pizza, the predictable presence of McDonald's, and a promising sounding taco shack called Manos Molena's. My pockets are full of American dollars and traveler's checks, though I'm adding little to the local economy so far. I've avoided the easy sleep offered by the Pisco Sours, and I'm not hungry for Peruvian tacos yet. I'm hoping I can hold out until the menu is more indigenous further inland.

I'm on a subsidized road trip, a personal and professional pilgrimage paid for by an anonymous donor. It's spring break, and my tab's being picked up to journey for a week with my student Thomas Pierce. For eight months, Thomas, a Wofford senior, has circled the globe on the one of the best undergraduate deals in the US. Each fall, one Wofford student is tapped by the college president, deemed "most likely to benefit humanity," and given a budget to plan seven or eight months of travel in the developing world. With the assistance of an advisor, this "presidential scholar" then formulates a topic he or she will explore for the duration of the trip. Sometime during the trip, the advisor or other faculty member is set out to rendezvous with the scholar for a week, a sort of "mini" scholarship of its own. We choose to meet in Peru, which writer Hugh Thompson claims now occupies the place in the popular imagination once held for Tibet, and where he claims in the opening sentences of *The White Rock: An Exploration of the Inca Heartland*, "the imagination is licensed to allow all manner of utopias and adventure."

Since I saw him last, Thomas has become steeped in adventure and has a notion or two about utopias as well. He is exploring the idea of intentional communities, and that topic has taken him to the isolated rainforests of Papua New Guinea (which he always shortens to PNG) to look at a network of native villages held together by an organic coffee co-op, to intentional communes in India, a Buddhist community in Thailand, a self-sufficient settlement in South Africa, "eco-villages" in Senegal, and a rainforest tourist "eco-camp" in the Peruvian Amazon. Tomorrow, in the high Andean city of Cuzco, he'll meet me and we'll hike, bus, and float through the valley of the Rio Urubamba all the way to legendary Machu Picchu.

Thomas's trip has been eventful so far. In October, when he left South Carolina, the history and English major was stopped by Homeland Security and not allowed to board his flight because of a suspicious looking box he was carrying. It was a small replacement pump a field biologist in PNG had requested to repair some research equipment. Thomas had all the right papers, but something looked fishy to the clerk about the metal pump—or the bearded student with the backpack. They sent him home.

A week later, when his airliner was tossing violently in the sky over the Pacific on the way to Port Moresby in PNG, he was sure that the Homeland Security delay had killed him. His flight was diverted to Japan, and when they landed he found out they'd flown through a typhoon. He spent several days in the terminal waiting for another flight to PNG, and he had plenty of time to think about the complex nature of scholarship and world travel.

A month later, when Thomas arrived to India, he rented a bay-side hut on stilts with a mattress near Auroville, India. He rode a scooter around, walked on the beach, interviewed several holy men, and lived on rice and fresh fish. Seven days after he left Auroville, the vast tsunami of December 26, 2005, wiped out the village. By that time, Thomas had arrived in Thailand and was staying an hour north of the resort towns flattened by the tsunami that day.

If all this was not enough to mess with the head of a young traveler, as Thomas was preparing to leave Thailand for Africa, he received word that the friendly (though alcoholic) bush pilot who had flown him into his PNG village destination had died in a crash when his small plane nosedived into a jungle mountain. Thomas, a regular in the theater productions back home, reported by e-mail that he felt he was being pursued by some great storm of misery, like something out of Greek tragedy imagined by Sophocles, and that he had barely remained one step ahead of where the great global hammer of fate would next drop.

Twenty years ago when "the donor," as everyone refers to him, gave Wofford this round-the-world scholarship, he is said to have wanted the presidential scholars to feel like they were going to war for a year, so he must be very proud of Thomas. The donor knew that to send an undergraduate student off alone into the developing world with cash, traveler's checks, an American Express card and a backpack is risky, but it is the closest they would get to combat. This was long before 9/11 and the War on Terror and Iraq and Afghanistan made war real once again for Thomas's generation. The college has continued to carry out the donor's instructions, though these days the administration works to find "host country" contacts for each stop. If not "safe," the trips are at least a little more predictable.

For over twenty years, the scholars have departed, experienced initiations and challenges unavailable to their peers, and returned to the campus for their senior year to talk about their trip to anyone who would listen. Thomas says the donor's instructions are clear and concise—live simply, keep your eyes open, travel light, and experience "it," the full body slam of world culture available to you once you get off the beaten tourist track.

Sitting in Lima on the eve of my week of presidential-scholar adventure, I've got some departure anxiety of my own. I envy Thomas's youth. It gets harder to "vacate" every year older I get. All the way into my forties, unmarried, blissfully ignorant of responsibility, I lived mostly out of the back of my pick-up, and one place or destination was just about as good as another. Though I had a year-to-year job teaching at Wofford, I never really settled, didn't look at it as a career, and I waited around, expecting a big strike in the creativity lottery—a novel, a substantial book of prose, a big prize that would set me up and apart and reveal my "true" calling to the world. In my mid-forties, I suddenly grew up and realized the big strike might not happen, took my job seriously, finished an advanced degree, received tenure, got married, built a house, took on the responsibility of loving a good woman, raising two boys, and caring for where I've been planted.

So one reason for the "pre-departure anxiety" might be that I actually have a home to leave, a place and people I truly care about. I have practiced the rituals of departure most of my life. Now it's the rituals of settlement that fill me up most often—coffee in the morning in a familiar cup, the discipline of daily writing, walking the same trails with the dogs behind our house. Just before I drove to Charlotte to catch my late afternoon flight to Lima, I kissed Betsy, then both the dogs. I said goodbye to the two boys watching TV downstairs, though I didn't try to kiss them. That would have been a little too much, even though I would have liked to.

It's now 2:00 A.M. and I'm settled here in Lima at least for the next seven or eight hours until my flight to the Andes. Though I am stretched out with my pack for a pillow, there are hundreds sitting upright, gathered around small tables eating and talking. There's a quiet murmur, and in the cavern of the concourse it sounds a little like a hive of bees. It's possible to believe, like a species of insects, we're all related, a swarm of travelers settled down for the night, all here for similar reasons, but with an ethnographic glance I quickly sort those sprawled in the food court into two distinct types with different goals and expectations concerning Peru: there are those, like me, on an "Inca pilgrimage" to Cuzco and Machu Picchu, dressed in our Eddie Bauer or Mountain Hardware fleeces and hiking boots and sunhats, carrying expensive backpacks and walking sticks, our sunglasses dangling from Croakies around our necks; in contrast to us pilgrims, there is a large US teenage mission group led by two middle-aged men with "youth minister" printed on their matching hats. I don't talk with them but imagine they are fulfilling a holiday faith commitment to save Peruvian souls and build houses in the suburban slums of Peru.

Right next to where I'm laid out a pod of these quick-hit teenage missionaries sit on their overstuffed rolling Samsonite luggage and sing and play a mournful folk song about "the Rapture" on guitars. "I wish they'd all been ready," they harmonize, leaning into the circle with their instruments. I call it folk music, but it's only that in three-chord structure and the tempo. It's the new protestant church music in its meaning and message, and because of that, it turns me off.

I've grown judgmental as a Pharisee about religion and don't think much of either the message or the meaning of the touring evangelicals. I'm off to deepest Peru to briefly touch the old and enduring pagan shadows of Indian America I know survive in the Andes and the Sacred Valley of the Inca—what poet Gary Snyder calls "the Old Ways"—and it's thrown me off a little that the missionaries are headed into the interior as well. "Pilgrimage is premised," Rebecca Solnit suggests in *Wanderlust: A History of Walking*, "on the idea that the sacred is not entirely immaterial, but that there is a geography of spiritual power."

But it's not pilgrimage that brings these teenagers out of the suburbs of Columbia, South Carolina, to the coastal plain of Peru, it's a mission from some God hungry for converts that pulls them for a week from their suburban homes and schools. A mission is premised on an operational task like saving souls. It has a slight military tone and a strict sense of success or failure and summons in my mind a junior officer reporting, "Mission accomplished, sir." I see from their uniform, their matching yellow tee shirts, that this group is from a church only ninety miles from my home. Agree with their mission or not, we have so much in common—we are mostly white, middle-class South Carolinians of the early twenty-first century. I know the chances are that at least a handful of these young Christians could end up at the college where I teach, and one of them, if they're lucky and brave and smart, could end up the Presidential Scholar.

Which is sillier in the end, my pagan pilgrimage or their Christian mission? They haul the Word of God around the planet and build a few prefab houses. On our trip we will be looking for a glimpse or two of the old gods as we hike a few trails. Why has scorn for conservative Christians replaced tolerance in my spiritual toolkit? Part of it is a sort of hardening of my spiritual arteries. In my twenties, I ceased to believe in organized religion. With no family to raise and my life on the road, I had no need for a home church, no interest in communing with those who put settlement above experience, faith above reason, man above nature. Like many in literature, I abandoned theology for myth, "the Greatest Story Ever Told" was replaced by Joseph Campbell's "myths to live by." Sleep being at a premium in the noisy terminal, I have plenty of time to close my eyes and reflect on all this and its soundtrack, the chorus of sincere young voices.

Along with my settlement five years ago came little of the ritual often associated with it. Though we're a Southern family we don't go to church, or read the Bible, or vote for politicians who talk of family values or guarantee relief of our "tax burden." I was born in the Southern church, but I still do not live in it. Funerals, christenings, and weddings are the only ceremonies I attend.

For decades, travel to wild places was my church. I have no belief in God as these young missionaries would define it; instead I share an "allegiance with the mystery of life" as writer Barry Lopez put it as he stared out at the sea filled with life, ice, and water in *Arctic Dreams*. My spiritual life is not portable like these Christian folk songs. It is wild and place-based and hard to access. It is stumbled upon on Wyoming mountain trails and sloshed through in Florida cypress swamps and accessible in the sudden presence of a moose on a river bank in Maine, or it is spotted just for an instant tumbling over the horizon line of a Mexican waterfall. There is no denying it once it approaches and no forgetting it once it arrives.

Once I went to a lecture by a photographer who'd spent ten years photographing sacred landscapes from the air in a Cessna—the solstice bird and the great triangle of the Nazca in southern Peru, Mayan ruins in the rainforests of Yucatan and Chiapas, standing stones in Britain, and California's

Winterhaven-stickman and effigy mounds strewn across the American landscape of California and Ohio. The photos in her black-and-white photography book often treat the subject landscapes in shadow, the angle of the plane, altitude, and time of day, and there is always something haunting about the sites. They reveal, as one of the book's commentators suggests, that "earth and man are of the same essence." As the artist clicked through her set of slides, she commented on how each image represents the shutter of her camera open for only a brief moment, and added together the time of exposure for all the photos in the book is less than a minute.

As we sat in the dark and studied landscapes sacred to thousands of people, long dead, she mused how ten years of her life is unaccounted for in the sequence of photos—the sorrow of a divorce, two boyfriends, and a thousand advertising jobs making a living with a camera. "It doesn't seem to matter," she said. "These images always redeem that lost time."

II.

Seen from 14,000 feet, the city of Cuzco, ancient capital of the Incas, is marked by its great colonial square and the sprawling red Spanish tile roofs laid out in the Andean Valley several thousand feet below. Landing, the plane does a corkscrew to hit the runway with the wind in the right direction, and all around the shadow-creased Andes form walls to climb for any escape. Thomas meets me at the airport looking like a young Bob Dylan. After eight months on the road, he's taken to cutting his own hair. "So it's Dylan and his sidekick Wordsworth," I joke, "off on a week of pilgrimage in the Andes."

We cab downtown and through the Plaza de Armas with its sixteenth-century cathedral built from the stones of the

Incan palaces that fronted it in pre-Spanish times. The cabbie points out the huge Incan stones that the earthquake of 1950 exposed under one of the big churches. The way history is faulted and twisted here is almost geologic, and I'm filled with the thrill of "deep time" all around me.

Thomas seems road-wise and comfortable with the daily weather of travel. He's found a good cheap hotel just off the plaza, and the cab drops us out front as he bargains with the driver in Spanish securing a reasonable fare. The room is small with two single beds but cozy. When we settle in, Thomas flips open the laptop he's carried around the world and plays the one CD he listens to over and over, *Mermaid Avenue*, unrecorded Woody Guthrie songs as interpreted by Billy Bragg and Wilco. I ask him about one of the songs, "Airline to Heaven," and he repeats the lyrics like a poem: "Them's got ears, let them hear. Them's got eyes, let them see. Turn your eyes to the Lord of the Skies. This airline plane. I'll take you home again to your home behind the skies."

Though religious, Guthrie's lyrics are a sharp contrast to the Christian music I heard in the airport. I lean back on the pillow, listening to Guthrie's 1930s Popularism filtered through WTO protests, and Thomas talks about his trip. He tries to explain how there's the trip on the itinerary—the outer series of events, experiences, encounters—and then there's what happens inside after so much time on the road, living out of a backpack. His time alone it seems has thrown shadows on the adventure. It hasn't all been good. "On a trip like this, the realization emerges that all of your habits and thoughts, your personality, are just patterns. That's a rough moment." He leans back listening to Billy Bragg. "Sometimes, I could almost step outside myself and watch as I reacted and interacted in predictable ways. I felt like a prisoner of my own chemistry. Though it's a scholarship, the trip is not an exercise of the mind. It's helped me realize the mind is unreliable and that I have to appeal to something larger and external to me for understanding. I was 'under-mined,' you might say." Then he thinks for a moment and calls the Presidential Scholarship "the pedagogy of ordeal and exile."

Could I do it? I don't think so. Not now, and maybe not even then, thirty years ago when I was Thomas's age. In some strange way, he seemed older than me, more experienced, as he talked about traveling around the world alone on the ultimate circumambulation. I listened to Thomas talking a few minutes longer, and then I fell asleep for my first night in the Andes. Outside the window a captive green parrot in the courtyard screamed a series of English words, "Hi! Come here! Go away! Stay back!"

III.

Two days later, we're climbing out of the bowl of the city on a second-class bus, headed up and over the near ridge to the village of Chinchero, a brief stop on the tourist road to the valley of the Rio Urubamba, known, the tourist guides say, for its hand-woven Incan textiles. We plan to hike from Chinchero down a small tributary of the Urubamba, following the route of the old royal Incan road from Cuzco. The bus route hugs a larger creek drainage leaving this old section of the Incan road isolated for miles miles down the valley.

We arrive late in the day and find the one hostel in town, get a room, wander down to the village square just as the last of the tourist buses leave for Cuzco. To the west is the high range of the Andes, and the sun sets slowly behind them. The little Spanish church at Chinchero is built on the foundation of an Incan villa, and the valley of the small creek we'll follow in the morning down to the Urubamba is stair-stepped with old Incan terraces. I look closely at the huge square stone I'm sitting on, and it's carved with a spiral and orange lichen grows in the groove.

We head down the valley and sit on a stone couch the Incas carved facing the sunset. I settle back and take it in and think that this is one of those perfect moments—sunset, mountains, cloud ranges catching the last strong sprays of the pink light. Behind us in the creek valley, we'll walk tomorrow morning until we can hear the tapping of hammers of archeologists restoring a section of the Incan highway from Cuzco to Machu Pichu. They work protected under tents, replacing the old paving stones, shaping up the roadbed of one stretch of royal road that time and frost heave have disrupted.

Just as it seems possible to get lost in our own Peruvian adventure, our own thin slice of time complete with archeologists, a tiny young Quechua woman in traditional dress appears around the corner. She smiles, revealing no front teeth. Her hair is deep black, tied in braids linked behind her back. She waves to us and walks over. We stand to talk. "Bonita," she says, pointing to the sun. Thomas tries a little more Spanish, but Spanish is her second language, and so it's limited like ours. We communicate with a series of smiles and isolated words and gestures. We do find out her name is Tonya, and it seems so out of character here in the Andes, more like the name of some teenage Carolina girl on the mission trip to Lima. It's clear Tonya sells belts and cloth in the square to the tourists, and she points and communicates she's headed home on the narrow trail along the creek valley. She pulls out the woven belts, and we soon realize we are her last transaction of the day, so we each buy a belt and she shows us how to tie them in the traditional knot to keep them snug.

But then she doesn't leave. It's obvious she's not going home, even though she'll be walking in the dark soon. She picks a lavender wildflower from beside the trail and holds it up to the cloth she's woven. The colors match. We get it, in spite of the language barrier. This is where Tonya's colors come from, picked from the valley floor of her home, the yarn dyed in vats of local color. Then she plucks a handful of dusty gray mint and crushes it and rubs it over her face and gestures for us to do the same thing. We do and the mint is soothing to my skin.

We follow as Tonya walks the ancient narrow trail down into the valley floor where a small creek comes out of a thicket of eucalyptus and a crease in the hillside. The stone pavement of the old Incan royal highway cobbles the ground. There is a huge boulder we've not seen before, and the little creek flows under it. Tonya leads us behind it, and then we step up into the stone itself. We see then the Inca have carved it with seats and a passageway, and the creek washes the whole encounter with sound.

Once we're all three inside the boulder, Tonya points up to a condor the Incan artists have found in the stone itself, the wings sweeping bulges of stone above the carved doorway, the beak a carved point of rock. The carving speaks directly to the religious mystery around us. It is like stained glass or paintings of saints. I think of what Pablo Neruda saw in the carved condors 40 miles away at Machu Picchu. The carvings are where "the mother of stone and the sperm of the condors" meet.

We slip on through the carved passage and exit on the other side, step over the small creek, and we're back on the trail. Tonya circles us back up toward the high-carved perch where we were watching the sunset when she arrived. We all three sit down on the bench and watch the final light disappear behind the peaks.

Sitting here in silence as deep as any church, I realize she's circumambulated the sacred stone with us, and I briefly remember our hike in California three years before through the John Muir Woods, the summer after Thomas was a freshman. That time we'd circled Mount Tamalpais, and it had taken all day. It was planned, a pilgrim route suggested by famous poets. This act of circling is entirely unexpected. It grounds me in what I came to find, the great mystery of place.

The next morning we get up early on the misty ridge Chinchero straddles and stroll through the village, beginning our walk toward the distant valley of the Rio Urubamba. We wander down a narrow muddy alley that looks like it might take us to the far hillside and the trail, but we run into a dead end where the lane peters out. Outside a small store, we meet a local labor organizer named Fidel and a few field laborers gathered for a morning discussion. The men are dressed in old slacks and threadbare shirts and, in contrast to the three or four distinctive styles of hats favored by Andean women, wear plastic ball caps like you'd see in the agricultural South of the United States. Three-quarters of the original Incan fields are now fallow, but these men still carry short heavy hoes for working plots of potatoes among the terraces. We could be intruders, but they don't eye us suspiciously. They smile and treat us as guests. Fidel senses we are lost, stops what he is doing, and draws us a map of the route to Urquilla on one of his labor brochures.

Below us, in the descending creek valley, is the tent where the archeologists work to restore the old highway. It is too early for the tapping of their hammers. Coming toward us on the trail are two young brown boys herding two steers. Ahead of us, the narrow trail hugs the valley wall and winds down toward the Rio Urubamba six miles distant.

We walk two hours in the cool morning air past freshly ploughed fields first cultivated by the Incas two thousand years ago. When the trail finally peaks at the junction of two valleys, we get our first glimpse of the Rio Urubamba and our destination, the village of Urquilla eight hundred feet lower on the valley floor.

The Rio Urubamba carves north, the high brown roiling current visible even from here. It's bound for Amazonia two hundred miles distant and ten thousand feet lower. The Incas saw mountains as holy, but we have lost sense of how.

Ahead of me, Thomas takes one more step in his year-long circle back home to Spartanburg. I follow him down the trail. I came in search of pagan wisdom, but what little I've found is elusive. It would be much easier to go to missionary churches in the villages and sing protestant hymns familiar from my childhood. As I walk the rest of the Urquilla trail, I construct what little of the native religion I remember from books and fragmented encounters with the land and people like Tonya. "In South America," Hugh Thompson writes, "it's sometimes easier just to give yourself over to the unknown and see what happens."

We stop where the trail switches back, then descends steeply the remaining mile into the valley. We drop our packs briefly to the trail to rest our shoulders. From below, in the distant village of Urquilla, a strange modern music rises from this time not theirs. Thomas stands, shoulders his pack, and descends toward the valley floor. We carry this place with us in our blood, in the spaces the oxygen fills in as we descend. I see what looks from this distance like swarms of jade against the eucalyptus trees. There are wild green parrots massing in the valley below. Maybe the squawk of parrots is what I mistook for music.

It's dusty as we walk the steeply descending trail. I lean back and slip on loose cobbles rounded by some great past glacial atonement when ice covered these dry Andean valleys. If stones have memory, what is there left for us to know? How to stay upright on the journey is a beginning. I lean into the descent and find better footing.

IV

Even the upper end of the river
believes in the ocean.
—William Stafford,
from "Climbing Along the River"

GRADIENT

I'm up in Maine to paddle whitewater, and my friend Frank
Burroughs has it planned: we'll take two canoes with us for my
first excursion into the North Woods, several hours up the
Kennebec from his house near the coast. Frank's crafts of
choice for the trip are the functional fast Kevlar model and the
heavily rockered 15-foot wood-and-canvas Maine Guide canoe,
called a Templeton or a Comstock, built for Frank by Fred
Reckerds near Rockwood, Maine. The wood-and-canvas canoe
was developed in Bangor, Maine, during the 1870s based on
Penobscot birch-bark canoes, and the construction principles
are similar—thin, flexible ribs and planks covered with canvas
instead of bark. In Maine, people still paddle them, though in
the Southeast where I'm from you're more likely to see a
wood-and-canvas canoe in the rafters of a summer-camp
dining hall or pressed into service as a salad bar in the
occasional backwoods roadhouse.

Frank has rigged his garage for the storage of the canoes.
He has three, one a light, modern Kevlar model and the other
two the beautiful wood-and-canvas Maine Guide canoes. His
boats are lovingly maintained. As we survey his collection, I
see that there is space for one more canoe in the rafters just in
case the need or opportunity arises to acquire another. I have
no doubt that in Frank's mind the space will be filled with
wood and canvas. These lovely craft are an anachronistic habit
of mind Frank doesn't seem predisposed to abandon.

When I stare into the rafters of Frank's garage at his
wood-and-canvas canoes, I admit they puzzle me. They are the
sort of craft phased out at summer camps before I was born,
when aluminum took over the canoe business after World War
II, and yet here they sit in Frank's garage, stored carefully,
maintained exquisitely, and as he reminds me, paddled

frequently. I know that part of my bemusement is practical. An aluminum canoe, like the battered one I own down south, can lean, oxidizing, against an outside garage wall, home to possums, but a wood and canvas canoe, like a good guitar, calls to be put to use and has to be kept out of the weather.

Frank's two wood-and-canvas canoes call my own loyalty to watercraft into question. I'm a generation younger, and I grew up paddling whitewater in metal and synthetic boats, beginning with aluminum, which was soon replaced with plastic, fiberglass, and more recently, Kevlar. I've bumped over rocks and dragged boats through cobbles and gravel patches with no concern for damage to my craft. Paddling with Frank this week, I will not have the luxury of contemporary sloppiness. Every bump of Frank's canoe, during carry or paddle, will be noted, if not by a smudge on the white canvas bottom, then by Frank himself, who will fix the boat before it's returned to the rafters.

Though Frank and I are both writers, we are very different in our paddling and prose styles. Frank's sentences are elegant and dense. His output is measured. He's published only two books in twenty years. I'm prolific. My writing is more like a spring river in full flush. It's in the area of subject matter that we tend to converge. We both have written books about floating Southern rivers and collections of reflective essays with human culture and natural history at their often-watery cores. When we get together, every year or so, we end up paddling and talking more about canoes than we do writing. Looking up into Frank's rafters, I realize it might be the same thing—writing and paddling. Frank does everything with the same balance of practicality and joy that I see displayed in the rafters of his garage.

I have an afternoon and then a full day before my flight back to South Carolina. Today, Frank wants to introduce me to the ancient art of canoe poling, and so we'll take the two boats up, drive a logging road to where it ends at a put-in called Spencer Stream, and pole a little in the class-I ripples on a river ominously called the Dead. Next day, we'll get a local guide to shuttle us back to Spencer Stream and paddle tandem in his wood-and-canvas canoe sixteen miles from the put-in to the Dead River's confluence with the Kennebec at the Forks.

Preparing to leave Bowdoinham, I help hoist the Kevlar canoe out of its rack in the rafters, and then Frank lowers the bow of the canoe on pulleys from the ceiling. He slides the stern from its high crosspiece and settles the boat on his shoulders and the center paddling thwart. Walking with the canoe he looks like some sort of Greek monster with two legs and a humongous beak and crest. The Reckerds (he often calls the boat by its builder's name) rocks on his hidden shoulders as he crosses between the early sun and me. After a short walk Frank slides the canoe on the Chevy truck racks and ties it down. I've learned to stop asking if I can help. At sixty-one, Frank loves to do it himself, a necessary selfishness of an aging canoeist.

The canoe, like corn and the Clovis point, is a product of the new world. The force at work on the aboriginal mind to shape the canoe was most likely travel of differing distances, some of them quite epic. In the Southern piedmont and mountains, travel, even for the aboriginal populations, was essentially trail-walking, so we as adaptive souls had little trouble taking to the interstate highways.

Gradient was to be avoided in laying out trails. The earliest ones followed the contours of hills and hopped from valley to valley through gaps. Traveling game originally sought the ease of low gradient, and so 12,000 years ago early hunters tracked their prey and adapted these passages. The car, as anthropologist Edward T. Hall suggests, evolved as an extension of the feet, a certain sort of dream in men's minds. The interstates followed, extending the trail to rubber tires and petroleum. Canoes and rivers interest me more than cars and highways, though much of my time is spent driving interstates to reach rivers and the places where boat access is easy (Put-ins we call them now.).

From the St. Lawrence river southward on the Atlantic slope, dug-out canoes (the aboriginal word "kenu" means dugout) were also used for travel and war. Some were over one hundred feet long, hollowed from the single trunk of a pine, poplar, or cypress. Mostly dugouts were heavy, but some were also so small it's said a woman could heft one on her back and walk from stream to stream. These canoes were hollowed out by fire and ax and on the coasts often painted bright colors. Huge painted dugouts carrying twenty-five paddlers on each side and up to eight-five warriors attacked De Soto in the 1560s, mixing beauty and death.

Travel was something that was not to be taken lightly in the cold and rocky Northern waters where the birch-bark canoe developed thousands of years ago. As a combination of elements goes, cold and water can be deadly. Two paddlers in a canoe upset far from shore might have five minutes of clear panic before the bliss of hypothermia overcomes them. On a river, in rapids crazy with spring rains, the canoeist might face similar conditions complicated by rocks and current. In all high country, gradient is a given consideration as a river flows toward the coast. The trail, one could argue, led to the interstate, the foot to the wheel, but the river trails still offer in most places their primary courses, and the canoe is an original human response to those conditions.

From Labrador to Alaska, as far north as Kodiak and south, continent wide, until the diminished size of the white birch limited its production, the birch-bark canoe appeared as a response to the landscape. There is a sophistication, a maturity, to canoe design. The bark canoe is seaworthy enough to endure waves of large lakes and tides, light of draft enough to glide through the shrunken rivers and streams of midsummer, capacious enough to carry a large load on a long expedition, easy to repair, and light enough to portage. No doubt there is beauty in its long lines. High in quality of material and workmanship, the birch-bark canoe took on different forms. Near the mouth of the Yukon River, where there is turbulence, the craft was pointed at both ends like a kayak and even partially decked. In eastern Canada, the bow and stern of the canoe were raised and rounded.

A bark canoe's skin consists of large strips placed over a skeleton of spruce ribs. The decking fits the shape, the craftsman working from the outside in. No nails are used, the technique predating metalworking. Gravity, spruce gum, and for lashing, the roots of the white pine are all the nails that are needed.

It's not far from bark to the natural ingredients Frank prefers and preserves in his paddling preferences—wood and canvas. It's definitely less of a leap from birch bark to a wood-and-canvas canoe than from wood and canvas to aluminum, sort of like the distance between a turned maple bowl and a beer can.

As we'd stared up into the rafters, Frank had qualified his attraction to wood and canvas. It's more, he'd said, than their Luddite appeal. Wood-and-canvas canoes, he explained, have the best balance "between rigidity and flexibility of any material." Wood and canvas, he'd said, is surprising in this way. "The bottom can flex up three inches or more before ribs begin to splinter, if you are able to go over the rock at reduced speed." He pointed out this may be worth remembering as we work our way down the Dead.

After loading the canoes, we drive inland, following the Kennebec, one of Maine's biggest rivers. Although I only have a day and a half to burn in Maine's backcountry, Frank wants me to experience the river from the seat of one of his Maine Guide canoes. The two canoes—the Kevlar Mad River and the custom-made wood-and-canvas guide canoe—ride securely on top of his truck. As we drive, Frank explains the differences he sees in Northern and Southern canoeing. In the North, where the lightweight birch-bark canoe was developed, the canoe became an extension of the aboriginal and later the European culture. It was a working craft perfect for a land of lakes and rivers. "The norm up here," he explains, "was the long canoe trip involving a lot of rough water."

In the South, the wood and canvas, the industrial descendant from birch bark, was adapted as recreational equipment, camp gear, in the 1920s. These recreational wood-and-canvas canoes were kept at mountain-lake cottages and summer camps all along the East coast. In the Southern Appalachians, adventurous camp directors and canoe instructors developed whitewater programs and paddle the boats on local rivers. From his base of operations at Camp Mondamin for Boys and Greencove for Girls, Frank Bell, Sr., explored many of the whitewater rivers in the Southeast from the seat of a wood-and-canvas canoe as early as the 1920s. By the late 1950s canoe instruction and programming at a half-dozen camps—with legendary instructors like Fritz Orr, Sr., Ramone Eaton, John Delabar, and Hugh Caldwell—, included ambitious whitewater trips on the Nantahala and Chattooga Rivers. Frank says he took philosophy classes in the early 1960s at Sewanee University from Hugh Caldwell and finds it strange that as a student he had been unaware of his professor's summer employment in the mountains east of Sewanee as a whitewater canoe instructor and explorer of many of the region's now-premier whitewater runs.

It's ironic, I point out, how Southern suburban children in the 1950s and 1960s were exposed to running whitewater at summer camps, and from there it was only a short distance to an Atlanta poet and advertising executive, James Dickey, imagining four suburban men with canoes tied to the roof of their International Scout heading into the Southern mountains for a weekend of retreat and adventure that ends so famously tragically in the novel *Deliverance*. The men living in rural Maine would never be so unfamiliar with their rivers as Dickey's locals seemed to be, Frank says, and in 1960 wood-and-canvas canoes in the backyards we are passing would have been as common as bass boats.

Frank's right. To the locals up here, we might not look as much like Burt Reynolds and the boys to the rural folk we pass with these canoes on the truck. I can tell he doesn't like the comparison. There's something he's cultivated in his love for boats and boating that's in a different watershed than what's driven millions upriver to float down various "*Deliverance* rivers" all over the country since 1972. Paddling is craft—even art—to him. When Frank describes paddlers he makes distinctions such as, "He's an experienced paddler but not a good paddler." As I listen, I wonder what sort of canoeist I'll look like to him by the end of the trip.

Midday we arrive at the Forks, the confluence of the Kennebec and the Dead, a timber and fishing town now sharing space with raft buses and the business of industrial whitewater. One mile upstream from the Forks is Moxie Stream, a small turbulent tributary that freefalls toward the Kennebec. When we arrive at the junction of the rivers, Frank first drives me on up there to see some "kayaking water," a stair-stepping series of class IV–V rapids the locals like to run. In the pull-off, there is a truck with racks on top and two kayaks. "Manually propelled ATVs," Frank says, joking about the tiny yellow-and-red boats as we pass.

Later, as we stand and look down at Moxie Stream, Frank wants to make it clear that it's not entirely on aesthetic grounds he prefers canoes over kayaks. It's practical. "A canoe is less able to handle extreme whitewater like this," he says. "But it is a lot more versatile. You can take long trips from it, fish from it, run moderate whitewater in it, and carry it around immoderate whitewater, stand up in it, pole it upstream." And the sport of kayaking has little connection now to its origins. As Frank puts it, "Kayaking is an art form enormously refined from some single aspect of its original purpose." Recreation, he says, taken one way, means going back to beginnings.

Even though I've kayaked for twenty years, I share some of Frank's disgust when the passion for new boat design and a higher degree of "playability" has led the industry of whitewater. When I see the tiny "play-boats" tied to the racks of young boaters, I see a sport with closer ties to surfing and skateboarding than to traditional canoeing. "Materials, design, and technique" are the elements one historian of whitewater delineates as the thru-line for whitewater boating from deep past to dawning present. As these elements changed, so changed the activity. When I began to paddle, kayaks were thirteen feet long, molded from cross-linked polyethylene plastic and designed primarily for "river-running." The crafts had rounded bottoms, no sharp edges or rails, and tips so sharp we used tennis balls on them to keep from impaling our paddling partners in eddies. And technique? To paddle a kayak safely downstream, you needed similar strokes to that of canoeing. Four basic strokes could get you in a kayak from put-in to take-out—forward, back, pry, and draw. The only technique specialized for the kayak was the Eskimo Roll, a way of righting the boat, but "rolling" was not essential for river running.

These days kayaks are designed for a host of "rodeo moves" with names that could be right out of gymnastics, rollerblading, snowboarding, skateboarding, or surfing: McTwist, pirouette, whippet, loop, airwheel, clean 360, cartwheel, flat spin, and olie. Many paddlers have abandoned rivers, instead spending all afternoon on one wave near a "park and play" spot.

Boats are so small they can now fit out of sight in the hatchback of an SUV. I've always felt I sound like a geezer when I begin to talk this way. Turning my back on modern boat design and use sounds to me a little like an old man longing nostalgically for the past. As what John McPhee in *The Survival of the Birch-Bark Canoe* once called "a canoe-man," Frank doesn't care for the little kayaks either, but I know from what he's said in the past that he believes nostalgia is a sort of selective amnesia. I like to think Frank's disgust is based more on aesthetic and moral grounds.

Late that afternoon, we drive the sixteen-mile gravel road to the confluence of Spencer Stream and the Dead. We'll leave from this put-in for our paddle back to the Forks tomorrow, but today, Frank wants to show me a little about poling in the Kevlar canoe. The road ends at the river-wide thirty-foot horseshoe Grand Falls, and it's there we take the canoe and pole off the truck and play for an hour or two in the fast water. "Canoe poling is like paddling in that it is self-evident and anybody can do it, but doing it well is another matter, and it's remarkable what a skilled person can do, upstream or down," Frank says. I watch as he stands in the canoe with the long aluminum pole in both hands like a thin jousting stick. Then, the pole extended hand over hand along the stream's rocky bottom, Frank effortlessly moves the canoe upstream across a tongue of fast water and into an eddy on the other side.

Then Frank does it again, climbing thirty feet up the small rapid toward the falls. I watch him several times as he sets his angle, acquires speed for the ferry, and leans slightly into the downstream pole and crosses the current. I'm not sure I can do it, though I know I will soon have a chance. As I watch, I try to figure out the advantages of poling over paddling and finally settle on the contact with the stream's bottom and the ability to climb small rapids effortlessly. Frank says the experts can pole up class-III whitewater and I'm sure it's true.

I'm not so sure I believe Frank's assertion that the technique is "self-evident" and worry I will make a fool of myself when he hands me the pole. The whole thing reminds me a little too much of my one attempt at punting on England's Cam River while in Cambridge the summer of the Carnival Against Capitalism. That long-ago afternoon I had little skill at moving the boat with any grace or accuracy in spite of hundreds of tourists all around for role models.

When I'm finally holding the pole and standing in the canoe, I find some of the basics of poling second nature—the angle I need to set for crossing the current, reading water, knowing where to enter the stream. It's the balance and where to place the pole that throws me off. I find myself hunkered in the boat in an attempt to lower my center of gravity. In five minutes of poling, my thighs and lower back are so tight I don't think I can survive very long. From shore Frank tells me to relax and stand up more.

After five or six attempts to climb the small rapid, I swing the canoe to shore and step out. I've poled successfully only in content not form. I've achieved my goal of poling upstream, but I can feel in my body how uncomfortable I've been the whole time. The Zen Buddhists never talk about "beginner's body," only "beginner's mind." Learning a new physical skill at forty-five is not a comfortable thing. I can see from my poling sampler that expert's status or even intermediate in this skill would be a lofty goal. Frank says it's been a great skill to learn in his late fifties and early sixties, and he says he's finally feeling comfortable with a pole in his hands. As we load the boat on the truck to drive back to the Forks, I'm thinking I'll be glad to get a paddle back in my hands tomorrow on the Dead in spite of the radical change in equipment I'll experience with the wood-and-canvas canoe.

Next morning we hire a local to shuttle Frank's truck back to the Forks. Once we're on the Dead, there will be no road crossings for sixteen miles. As we drive up, Frank points out that if something happens and we smash the boat up on the rocks we'll have to walk out a mile or so through the woods to get to the put-in access road we're now driving. This paddle will take me as deep into "roadless" as I've ever been in a watercraft. We'll have the river to ourselves though. We're paddling on one of the Dead's "low-water" days with only natural flow. None of the thrill seekers will crowd the river. On peak release days from April to October, the dam releases fifteen-hundred to fifty-five-hundred cubic feet per second. On these days the Dead is one of the most popular whitewater runs in Maine, with many of the ninety thousand who run the state's rivers each year floating it.

Our shuttle guide, a local store clerk from the Forks, drops us and our boats and gear at the put-in and wishes us luck. He drives away leaving us standing in the parking area. I'm a little self-conscious, dressed like a kayaker in spite of my change of craft for the day. I've strapped on my helmet, including dangling nose plug for rolling, pulled on my blue nylon dry top and my blue splash pants. Topping it all off are my bright blue rubber booties with white soles. Everything I'm wearing would have to be bought at a whitewater outfitters shop. When I go on a river, I'm always specialized, geared up for the sport I love. Frank, in contrast, could comfortably walk into a bait-and-tackle shop and buy a lure or two or paddle downstream in his canoe. He's dressed more like a Maine guide—heavy tweed wool pants, a plaid cotton twill shirt the collar of which has been worn down to white batting, and L.L. Bean duck boots. His only concession to the industry of whitewater is a gray Patagonia paddling jacket he says he acquired at a Friends of Merry Meeting Bay auction. Warming his head is a Duke Forestry School cap, a gift from his daughter who went there. In the wood-and-canvas Templeton are two Tide bottle bailers with the tops cut out, a fly-rod in a case, four paddles, Frank's big green dry bag with our lunch, my smaller one with paddling gloves, and a black kayaking beanie.

The raft companies headquartered at the Forks advertise this river as having the longest stretch of continuous whitewater in the East, and looking downstream from the put-in I can see why. The gradient is steady, and the stream's bed is thick with boulders. As we stand on shore, Frank points out how we'll work our way to the far shore for our descent through the first rapid, Spencer Rips. When I'd asked a kayaking friend who knows the Kennebec watershed about paddling the Dead on natural flow, he'd said, "Oh no. Way too bony." Frank seems to think it's just right though for what we want, a sixteen-mile run down to the Forks with conditions much like a trapper might have experienced a century before—enough water to float the wood-and-canvas boat, but the descent veritable math problem at every moment. Where to run though the cobbles? Where to find enough flow to make the gradient work for us? Sitting in the bow of the canoe on the Spencer Stream side of the river I'm already a little tired thinking how many choices we will have to make to get safely downstream. The river is fast, and it will be no pleasure float. I step into the canoe and sit in the bow seat, resting my feet on the varnished ribs of the bow with the planking underneath. The Templeton is a lovely craft, and I make my vow to the river gods to do my part to keep it in whole on this descent. We peel out into the current and work our way across to the other shore, and I look back upstream at Grand Falls and tuck the sound of its falling current into my memory.

Spencer Rips is a fast series of three-foot waves at the termination of a tilted cobble run. Frank says that in the eddy at the bottom the raft companies like the big class III–IV compression waves that form on the surface as the release passes over the rocky bottom here. It's a good indication they'll get their money's worth on the Dead. He reminds me again what we'll experience today is much more technical with less than one thousand cubic feet of natural flow spilling through boulder gardens that are pretty much continuous for sixteen miles. I realize as we work downstream it's the ultimate canoe run, especially in Frank's fragile wood-and-canvas canoe.

After we paddle through Spencer Rips, the first half of the Dead blurs into one continuous morning of whitewater. I know there are named rapids somewhere in the riverbed below us, but they are hard to pick out. I'm working so hard all I can do is recite what should be here—the Minefield, Humpty-Dumpty, the Basin, Elephant Rock. I've read the guidebook, and I know that Enchanted Stream enters the river from the left, and I want to see a tributary with such a mythical name, but the banks in the distance dissolve as I focus on the ten or twenty feet in front of the canoe.

From the stern, Frank sets the general course, calls out the direction we need to go, and I respond with my minor corrections using bow or cross-bow strokes. The Reckerds, the most heavily rockered of any of Frank's canoes, responds quickly to the corrections. I've heard canoe instructors joking how any tandem craft should be called "the divorce boat" since paddling one in whitewater is often fraught with conflict, but so far Frank and I make a happy old odd couple, and I honor his commands. I cherish the clear channel he always guides us toward. Only once do we hear the rifle-shot sound of a wood rib cracking as it comes into direct contact with a cobble in its path. Mostly we manage to keep the boat in the swift water and off the rocks.

Halfway down we need a break from the non-stop "reading" of the whitewater so we pull over in a big eddy and walk a mile along an old logging road. My land legs return quickly and so does my land mind. The contrast of the trail to the river is perfect for reflection. Watery road and logging road—each of them trails to somewhere interesting. I adjust my vision to terrestrial surprises and start to think horizontal again after a morning of looking for whatever challenge is out ahead. Frank points out there might be ruins along the way from the logging business that has been Maine's main industry since before Thoreau took his trip into the woods in the middle of the nineteenth century, but we see none of the crib work fallen into the underbrush. I comment that it's a young woods, its maples six-to-ten-inch girths thickly crowding the trail. Frank says they may be older than I think, that trees in the North woods don't grow as fast as those woods down South I hold up for comparison. After we head back for the river, Frank points out the fiddlehead ferns everywhere and how the markets back home in Bowdoinham will soon be full of them. Back at the boat, we eat our lunch on the bank next to a shaded eddy.

When we start down the river again, there is little space for reflection, but it creeps in anyway. I think about canoes and kayaks the rest of the way down. "Every force evolves a form," the Shakers say. There were many aboriginal responses to travel by water, each appropriate to the situation: the kayak and umiak, rafts of rushes lashed together and abandoned on the far side of a deep ford, hide boats stretched over frames of birch saplings, crude bark canoes constructed for single crossings and left for the return passage, loose windfall logs pointed for the other shore. To craft is to manufacture with care and attention to detail. To build a craft to survive is to know just how much attention a particular situation demands.

None of these watercraft, as far as the literature shows, were constructed for recreation as many kayaks and canoes today are. They were crafted for work of various forms—hunting, fishing, gathering, travel. Estimates are that an aboriginal kayak or birch-bark canoe may have survived five seasons or so under the pressures of utility, a dug out, many decades, particularly the cypress models of the Southern coast.

Paddling techniques can't be carbon dated, and there are no fossil remains, no artifacts. We can only extrapolate backward into the past from boat and paddle designs. Most paddles were built for power and speed—a tapered blade at one end, a grip at the other. In my living room, I have a five-foot aboriginal paddle carved from a single piece of tropical wood in Suriname. I spotted it stashed with one of two others in the bow of a 20-foot dugout. It was used, I observed, for drawing the boat to shore or emergency propulsion when the outboard failed to fire, and the boatman was forced to resort to the virtue of paddle and muscle.

Before outboard motors were affixed to the sterns of dugouts in the last surviving backwaters of boating, they would not have required a sophisticated array of strokes. A forward stroke purposely applied, a crude draw, and ruddering steerage would have sufficed in Suriname or South Carolina for moving the boat from point to point on a black-water river or a calm bay. Dugouts, as a cultural form, are stable craft, sitting steady in the water, but do not lend themselves to the rocky rivers. It is in these rocky rivers where the bark canoe proved valuable.

The first day in a canoe course you learn a canoeist's technique for making a boat go straight—the classic J stroke. The stroke could easily have been perfected in the far north by aboriginal paddlers crossing lakes in high winds, digging hard for each inch of forward momentum against the backdrop of birches and pines along the shore. The cross-bow draw I'm using to move us through rapids may have been discovered descending through gradient like the Dead's, one steep enough to wrap a boat around a long run of current and glacial till. Much of this is speculation, but speculation based on floating rivers like the Dead.

Almost five hours after we put-in at Spencer Stream, we approach Poplar Hill Falls, the last set of rapids before we reach our take-out near the Dead's confluence with the Kennebec. I look back from my bow seat and see the first concern on Frank's face. He says he wants to get out and scout this one, a formidable drop even at these low water levels. As we stand on the bank and look downstream, I can see the gradient is much steeper than the twenty-nine-feet per mile of what's upstream. At higher water levels, Poplar Hill Falls would be a solid class-IV rapid. Even with natural flow, I can still see large waves and holes particularly on the left side. Frank looks it over, and we both agree we should probably run left. The holes and waves are bigger there, but it's much less rocky, and the chance of flushing through upright is much higher. We don't think much more about it. We simply get back in the boat and push off into the current.

The roar of water falling over stone is distinct and drowns out what concerns I may have. Frank sets the line and we commit to the run. We are moving faster than we have all day. It's as if we're on a tabletop tilted downstream. Frank calls out "left" and "draw right," and we're in the middle of it, the water breaking over the bow of the canoe, but we stay upright. By the time we're through the worst our boat is practically swamped but afloat.

"This is the most like Southern whitewater of anything we've paddled today," I say to Frank who is bailing water with the Clorox bottle. "I'm exhilarated!"

Frank smiles. I can tell he's happy we're safely at the bottom, but I get the feeling Poplar Hill Falls was not his favorite part of the run. To revel in the adrenaline settling back to normal levels is a little too much like recreational rafting for him, too similar to those boys running waterfalls in their kayaks, to those tourists who come on fat release days to conquer the Dead. Frank revels in the work of bailing to keep us afloat just as he worked at the steady job of edging a wood-and-canvas canoe down the Dead like the old Northwoods trappers and traders used to do.

YOUGHIOGHENY

From the eddy above the Youghiogheny's Swallow Tail Falls, my guide Chuck Stump tells us about a boy who had fallen into the swirling reversal of water below us at the bottom of the eight-foot ledge of rock. The boy's parents had watched in horror from the park overlook as their son disappeared. Eighteen hours later, while his parents were treated for shock in a local hospital, divers found the boy shivering but safe on a shelf of rock behind the falls. He had sat there for almost a day staring through the falling water.

Near the beginning of my adventure on the Youghiogheny, I sit safely at the bottom of Swallow Tail Falls. I have avoided the fate of the little boy, skirting the crashing reversal of cold spring water. I've taken two strokes and dropped like a leaf over the lip of the falls. I felt the bottom drop away, and then as sudden as water down a drain, I was sitting safely in the calm eddy water below.

I look back upstream at the steady river as it pours over the limestone obstruction. My trip down the Youghiogheny is underway. In the next week, like the water, I will head downstream, covering fifty-nine whitewater miles of the Youghiogheny River's journey.

The day we arrived in the watershed, it had been raining for eleven days. As we approached Maryland's panhandle, there had been showers and occasional downpours. Along the roadside, tiny streams tumbled through cobbles. The leaves of oaks and maples sagged, sodden with rain.

When I was a young kayaker, I'd prayed for rain. I was drawn, as all those of my watery tribe, to rapids, spots of resistant rock like this one. But now forty-six, the responsibilities of teaching, writing, and home had seriously reduced my boating time. In the late 80s and early 90s, when I was in my thirties and paddling difficult whitewater like this regularly, I lost two friends to paddling accidents. Something about attending funerals can change a middle-aged paddler's approach to adventure sports.

When *National Geographic* called to ask if I'd like to take this assignment to paddle the river for a book called *Adventure America*, I hesitated. I'd never paddled the Yough, and I knew it was difficult. It had been several years since I'd attempted class-IV or -V whitewater, though I'd been a regular on difficult rapids for two decades. "What's the worst that can happen?" my wife Betsy had asked.

"Death is unlikely," I admitted. "Only one or two kayakers have died in the difficult water of the Yough in thirty years."

"Injury?"

"Maybe I'll blow a shoulder." I said. "But I can recover from that."

"You should do it," she said. "How often do you get a chance for National Geographic to pay for a week of paddling?"

So I committed. My paddling partner on this kayaking adventure is Watts Hudgens, a younger colleague at Wofford College. The term is over. The papers are graded. It's early June, and Watts, being a long-time boater, jumped at the chance to head for the hills of Maryland and Pennsylvania.

"The Yough," as the locals call it, is one of four powerful Appalachian rivers—the Youghiogheny, the Monagahelia, the Tygart, and the Cheat—that form the upper drainage for the Ohio River and ultimately join the Mississippi. Out of this wondrous marriage of Allegheny Mountains and water that shapes the corner of West Virginia, Maryland, and Pennsylvania also rise, just east, across the continental divide, the headwaters of the Potomac and the Savage Rivers, carrying water from Backbone Ridge to the Atlantic Ocean.

The Yough's headwaters form among bold springs and fern-studded seeps on the western slope of Backbone Ridge just above Silver Lake, an old resort a few hundred yards into West Virginia. Above Silver Lake, the river is small enough to step across and is home to native trout. Below the lake, it quickly leaves West Virginia behind and flows into Maryland, where beavers block the Yough's flow as it meanders through alder and maple thickets. Neat farms are its neighbors in the first 30 miles as the river keeps to the fertile valley between Backbone Ridge and Chestnut Ridge.

Before the river leaves the Appalachians downstream at South Connelsville, it has flowed through "the Tippy Top," "the Top," and the "Upper," three upper stretches of premier "advanced" white water; Lake Youghiogheny, a twenty-mile reservoir for recreation and power generation; "the Middle," a fast, isolated section; "the Lower," beginning in Ohiopyle, Pennsylvania, the most rafted section of river on the East coast; and "the Bottom," maybe the most beautiful of the river's reaches, a wide expanse of water and sky with long cobble shoals and occasional rapids as the river carves through Chestnut Ridge.

The human history of the Yough is as long and complex as one of the Upper Yough's rapids. Early Indians arrived around 8000 BC and by 1600 BCE the Monongahelas lived in the river drainage. No one really knows when or why they disappeared, but they left their name for the river the Yough joins at McKeesport, just downstream from Pittsburgh. By 1737, the Youghiogheny had appeared on a map. By the middle of the century early white explorers were pushing to the west.

George Washington first journeyed into the headwaters in 1753 as a young colonial militia lieutenant, and in 1754 he returned to explore the river by canoe in hopes of finding a water route to the west to develop into a canal. The French claimed the Ohio Valley, a vital link between Canada and New

John Lane

Orleans, and Washington believed controlling the Youghi-ogheny was key to curtailing the French's access to the drainage. The French had successfully established Fort Deuquesne at the site of present-day Pittsburgh, the confluence where the Monongahela and Allegheny form the Ohio.

In the opening battle of the French and Indian Wars, twenty-two-year-old Washington suffered his only military defeat when a detachment of colonial troops he commanded was defeated at tiny Fort Necessity in the "Great Meadow" in the Youghiogheny's watershed.

Settlers who followed Washington west settled in inviting valleys such as those found where Sang Run Bridge crosses the Youghiogheny. "Sang," or ginseng, a wild plant with a curative root, is said to have been common in the area. For the old-timers, hunting sang provided a steady cash crop—like vegetable gold. Today, whitewater outfitters have provided a new kind of gold for the hills of western Maryland.

With ample budget from National Geographic, I have arranged for two more guides, Steve Strothers and Terry Peterson, to meet us on our second day paddling. We are to meet them at 11:00 A.M. out in front of Mountain Surf, a kayaking gear shop in Friendsville, Maryland, the take-out for an 8-mile section known as the "Upper."

The scene in Friendsville is youthful, thick and electric, especially when the Upper Yough is running. Boaters who could just as easily be surfers or skateboarders hang out on the wall in front of Mountain Sports and watch for cars carrying kayaks. Everyone has a nickname. The chatter is relentlessly aquatic.

Steve and Terry lean against the wall in front of Mountain Surf. He works as a cartographer for the USGS in Washington, DC, but spends every weekend paddling the river three hours west of the capital. Terry offers a nice contrast to Steve. She floats the river full time, experiencing the Yough as both raft guide and kayaker. When we arrive, they report the river is higher than normal, with two feet of natural flow plus water released from the dam upstream at Deep Creek reservoir. To paddle or not? Steve suggests it is probably best to wait for the release from the Deep Creek Dam to pass.

We drive the ten miles upstream to Sang Run where we stand on the bridge and wait for the water in the river to drop some. Steve places sticks at the water's edge so we can know when the water has dropped enough to paddle. As we stand watching the river flow past, Terry explains the complex politics of the Upper Yough, how the access has always been contested, and only in the last ten years—when river conservation groups such as American Whitewater Association fought for the establishment of a Department of Natural Resources parking lot—has it become easy to leave a car at the top and put on the river with ease.

For years, the locals made recreational boating difficult. Gunfire was not uncommon on the Upper Yough. In the early days, rafters would stop on the bridge, throw their rubber craft in the river and climb down the bridge abutment as a friend drove the car away. "In the early days they'd bring me up here and show me the bullet holes," Terry says.

An hour later, when the sticks Steve has placed at the water's edge are high and dry, we know it is time to paddle. The extra water released from the dam had finally passed us. "That's about as low as it's going to get," Steve says.

A few miles below Sang Run Bridge, the Upper Yough takes on the character it is famous for—narrow, continuous, technical. The names of the rapids suggest the serious intent of the water: Bastard, Eddy of Death, Snaggle Tooth, Charlie's Choice and Triple Drop, Zinger, and Little Niagara, to name a few. "Exercise good judgment regarding your boating skills," one river guide urges. "Expertise, bravado, and life insurance."

"This is the most dangerous rapid on the river," Steve says as we enter a class IV–V rapid called Heinzerling. I follow Steve and Terry as they slip through an impossibly narrow blind slot into a big eddy shaded with sycamores. "If you didn't know that slot was there, you'd head right into the worst of it," Steve says, relaxing in the eddy.

As I sit in the eddy, I look over my shoulder and down comes a boater in a Kevlar wildwater boat with no paddle, only little black flippers on his hands. He is smiling as he goes straight through the forbidden passage Steve calls "the rifle barrel."

"That's Jeff Snyder," Steve says, smiling, "the father of squirt boating."

I know Snyder as one of the pioneers of paddling small kayaks through difficult whitewater. Steve does not seemed surprised to see him a boat that looks more like a huge cigar than a kayak.

"Does he do that often?" I say in disbelief.

"Unprecedented," Steve smiles. "Probably the first person ever to have done it."

I look over my shoulder. Down below the rifle barrel Jeff has the fat wild-water boat standing on its end as he slams against the pillow rock and rides the current down to the left.

Steve follows Snyder downstream. I watch his route, how he too rides up on the rock pillowed with water that had stood Synder's boat vertical. I shake my head. "They're doing that on purpose," I mutter. I take several strokes and shoot down the rifle barrel too and drop into twenty yards of impossibly chaotic, slanted exploding water, "the death slot" on the left, and the big pillow rock with a quarter of the river piling against it on the right. As I pop through the offset waves all I can see is the chaos below. I miss the pillow and somehow punch through the grabby hydraulics at the rapid's bottom.

It is in the class IV–V Heinzerling that I see most clearly how the dance of water and stone on a whitewater river speaks of danger. This slippery equation between challenge and risk is at the heart of adventure sports such as whitewater kayaking. When is a river too difficult? When is it best to stand on shore and admire a serious stretch of gradient? The lucky ones among us get to chase the answer down a wild rapid like Heinzerling and make it through.

Several miles downstream from the take-out for the Upper, the Yough disappears into 20-mile-long Lake Youghiogheny, finished by the Corps of Engineers for flood control in 1943. The lake, the only major reservoir on the Youghiogheny, provides recreation of a different sort. On any summer day, the whining of jet skis can be heard and expensive powerboats leave tracks in the jade-green water.

Our third day on the river, we stay just downstream from the Youghiogheny Lake dam at the River's Edge, a bed and breakfast in Confluence, Maryland, that caters to the outdoor tourists drawn to town by the river and the bike trail that terminates at the base of the dam. Just off the main street in Confluence, the Casselman, the Yough's largest tributary, joins with Laurel Hill Creek and the Yough to form what Washington and the early explorers called "the turkey foot."

Early in the morning, Watts and I switch boats, leaving our whitewater kayaks on the truck. We slip down the bank amid a din of indignant geese. Our blue and brown sea kayaks, longer and thinner than the whitewater boats, paddle straight with less effort on the flat water and still perform well in the five or six rapids we will descend.

Along the left bank of the Middle Yough runs the backbone of a contemporary recreational industry, a bike path stretching over fifty miles downstream, a hard-packed limestone trail set on the bed of an abandoned railway that made Washington's idea of a canal obsolete in less than one hundred years. The Middle Yough also carries recreational canoe traffic, mostly fishermen and low-intensity paddlers who want an easy run and pastoral scenery downstream from the Upper and upstream from the Lower.

As we float past "the turkey foot" on the dam release from Lake Youghiogheny, I think about Washington's first canoe trip downstream. Unlike us, the father of our country had big industry on his mind—a trade route via water to the Ohio River—and he probably could never have imagined such a confluence of modern recreational desires as we can see from the Middle Yough.

Washington's early Wilderness Road, what became known as the Braddock Road, was improved and rerouted to later become in 1818 the first federally funded highway. This highway, known as the National Road, ran from Cumberland, Maryland, to Wheeling, West Virginia. The road crossed the Youghiogheny just above the site of today's town of Confluence at an old ford called the Great Crossings. The bridge that was built for the National Road across the Yough is now below the waters of Lake Youghiogheny. Sometimes in October, if the water has been dropped far enough, you can see the three span stone bridge appear like a ghost from the nation's childhood just upstream of the present day Route 40 crossing.

Downstream is gorge country, with sharp Pennsylvania ridges descending one thousand feet to the river. If the Yough has a soul, it lingers in the broad peopleless floodplain within the horseshoe bend called Victoria Flats below Confluence where the coal-mining town of Victoria once stood. Just past two islands, we stop to look for the ruins of the old town. We find nothing.

Watts and I follow a tiny trail inland through dense spring wildflowers under sycamore and river birch. There are Jack in the Pulpit, and others. We climb the hill to a railroad and see five vultures take to the air from the fresh carcass of a white-tail deer killed by a train. As we walk the tracks, we notice that this is not uncommon, this collision of train and deer. The bones of another deer—a young male with spikes for a rack—rests less than twenty yards away.

Soon we are back on the water. Halfway from Confluence to Ohiopyle we pass into Ohiopyle State Park, a nineteen-thousand-acre preserve. Within the park's sanctuary, we drift downstream in our big boats. I go deep inside myself and think about things—waves, trees, the shore, the mountains beyond. The woods beyond the river are mostly second growth, trees thirty or forty years old, though Watts points out a huge cedar in the woods that could have seen centuries of water passing downstream.

Five more miles of fast flat water broken by occasional class-II rapids, and we see the Ohiopyle railroad bridge ahead. We step out of our boats with the eighteen-foot Ohiopyle Falls, just below. We stand on the fescue corner of the park's waterfront. Downstream, we can see nets across the river to catch any unaware boater who might float down from the Middle Yough toward the falls.

"There's no place like Ohiopyle, no place that even comes close," Tim Palmer wrote in his epic 1980s narrative *Youghiogheny: Appalachian River*. "All roads out of Ohiopyle are climbed in second gear. All roads into Ohiopyle burn the brakes." As we drag our boats up onto the grass, we can see what Palmer means. The green slopes of the Yough's formidable gorge slip down to the edge of the river on one side and on the other form the backdrop for parking lots and a few old buildings. There stands the old general store, now The Falls Store & Inn, several churches, a train station, and several dozen white clapboard houses.

Earlier in the week, I had commented to Watts on the young Upper Yough boaters in Friendsville with their trendy short boats, dreadlocks, and their ritual of hanging out at the wall in front of the Mountain Surf shop. I'd called it "the grunge capital of kayaking."

"These are my people," I say today, laughing as we pull our boats onto the grass in Ohiopyle, pointing at the cars parked in the private boaters' parking lot. On the boatracks are ten-year-old kayaks, long Perception and Dagger boats in discontinued colors. The boaters mostly look like middle-aged professionals out to red-line their excitement meters during a day off.

Ohiopyle has been a recreational bonanza, the rafting capital of the East, since the early 1960s. Because of the regular releases of water from Lake Youghiogheny the commercial rafting traffic can continue all summer when everything else in the mountains is dry. The power company regulates its release of water, and the state of Pennsylvania regulates the paddling in Ohiopyle. Five rafting companies operate there, with one-hundred thousand tourists a year parceled out between them, each company floating them down the eight miles of the exciting, though not usually pushy, Lower Yough.

It is easy to see that the anarchy and alchemy of Friendsville is far behind. The dam upstream of Confluence provides predictable daily flow all summer. On the Lower Yough, the private boaters must compete for several thousand permits, and launch times are assigned according to availability. Even "the shuttle" is complex and bureaucratic, a sharp contrast to the recently settled boating frontier just thirty miles upstream on the Upper. Private boaters in Ohiopyle must purchase a token to ride a bus back from the "take-out" to their vehicles parked a mile or so up the hill from the river.

The next day, we hook up with Laurel Ridge Outfitters for the 11:00 A.M. commercial trip down the Lower Yough. The river is a good level, almost three feet. The dam is releasing more water because of all the rain. I ask the manager of Laurel Ridge about our desire to paddle the last leg of the river down to South Connelsville, and he says, "You've got to go down with 'Cube,' a guide of ours who grew up on the river and fishes that stretch. I think he's got the day off."

He points to the staging area for the rafts. Cube is pumping up a raft. He has long grey hair pulled in a ponytail under his Lawyers.com cap. Cube agrees to meet us the next morning, saying that he will paddle down with us in his Shredder, an inflatable catamaran, a popular craft of local design.

"What can I expect of that final stretch?" I ask Cube. "You're gonna love it down there," he says, smiling. "No access except by river. It's bear and train country."

So the next day, our final on the river, is shaping up to be an adventure, with Cube as our guide. But first, the famous Lower Yough still awaits us. The Laurel Ridge trip has three rafts, fifteen brave adventurers. During the July-August "high season," the outfitter might have eighty people on a trip. These guests are mostly British from the Royal Air Force. "They come over every year," Bo Harshyne, the trip leader explains. "We had a group of pilots come over one year," Bo says. "You know, face plants on mountain bikes. You couldn't stop those guys."

We put on with the commercial trip in the pool below Ohiopyle Falls. There's a big bubble of water at the fall's base, and we work against the strong current to paddle up on top of it, but the current pushes us downstream. I think about how every October many local boaters run the falls on Falls Race Day.

Chuck Stump, our guide on the Top Yough, had said that this past year he ran it nine times in one day, and he couldn't understand why it wasn't open for business all year. "Over a thousand runs on the Falls Race day and nothing bad happened. I saw Jeff Snyder go over it standing up in an inflatable kayak."

We follow Cube's safety boat and the other rafts through Entrance Rapid, the first of a series of rapids along the famous "loop," an oxbow where the Youghiogheny doubles back on itself. The peninsula in the middle is called Ferncliff, a nature preserve and national natural landmark.

One of the RAF rafts flips in a rapid called Cucumber, and we can see yellow helmets and paddles bobbing in the froth ahead of us. The vacationing pilots are laughing as they float past.

I laugh too. Though not as difficult or exhausting as the Upper Yough, the Lower offers pure recreation. It feels good to be on the water, breaking through the waves and into the swirling eddies.

The river is perfect for whitewater recreation. It drops twenty-seven feet per mile from the bottom of the falls to Bruner Run take-out, eight miles downstream. There are thirteen named rapids, many of them class III, some even class IV at higher water levels. Many of the best drops are in the first mile of the river, and often kayakers will put in, run the loop, and then walk their boats across the peninsula and back to the parking lot.

Downstream for six miles after the loop, we float through standing waves and past big slabs of limestone. One rapid, a class III called Dimple, has claimed three lives in the last year, and I sit in an eddy impressed with the safety precautions Laurel Ridge Outfitters takes with their trip. The trip leader stands on top of the rock with a whistle, moving rafts like a traffic cop. All the Laurel Ridge rafts make it through, the RAF troops slapping paddles in the fast, constricted channel below the deadly undercut rock. Other outfitters are not so lucky. Five rental rafts with no guide—what the outfitters call "unguided missiles"—flip, some dangerously close to the rock. The rafters float downstream, paralyzed with fear. We watch as kayaks rush into the current and pull the bobbing boaters ejected from the raft into the calmer side eddies. Some customers, with no kayak to rescue them, float passively fifty yards downstream until they lodge like litter among boulders.

Finally out of the current, they flop like exhausted trout on sidebars of gravel.

It's quite a show. In spite of Dimple Rapid and its deadly reputation, one-hundred thousand people float the Lower Yough every year. All the way to River's End, the last rapid on the run before the take-out at Bruner's, I watch the faces of the British guests tilting their fun meters in Laurel Ridge's three rafts.

It is raining when the Laurel Ridge truck drops us off at the Bruner Run take-out for our final ten-mile float down the Bottom Yough to South Connelsville. This is where the Yough leaves the mountains behind. Just downstream from Bruner, the high tourist energy of the Lower section recedes into memory and river miles.

"If you focus on the right things, and ignore the others," Rick Bass wrote in his essay "River People," "you can find wildness and freedom anywhere, I'm convinced." Our final day on the river, I focus on what Cube calls "the wildest, most beautiful section of the Yough."

I can see Cube is right from our first moment. The ridges on the Bottom Yough are high and green, constricting the river into a tight gorge. The water is swift and pure. It is as if the landscape, in its last ten miles of mountain wildness, is intent on holding the river for itself. There are not rapids as long or difficult as we have seen upstream on the Top, the Upper, and the Lower, but there is something—call it isolation or distance—that makes the Bottom Yough feel freer than any stretch above it.

As we drift downstream, Cube and Watts paddle the black shredder out in front of me in a band of soft mist. Cube has his fishing rod with him, and in a broad eddy he casts into the current. The river has always provided. "Once I was sitting in this eddy," Cube says. "It was midday and I was hungry. The fish weren't biting." Upstream, floating down from the

Lower Yough like a tiny raft, was a bright red box, bobbing in the wave train. "The box floated into the eddy," he says. "It was a Tupperware container and inside was a full lunch just packed that morning."

By noon we have drifted through the last rapid before the industrial town of South Connelsville. We pull our boats out on a cobble beach where the local teenagers have positioned slabs of river-worn limestone to form a party bench, a real Fred Flintstone sofa.

Upstream we can see the Youghiogheny carving through the mountain gorge the tourists frequented. Downstream, Cube points out a boulder the locals call Turtle Rock. Generations of South Connelsville teenagers have painted the large boulder in a hundred different hues. It marks the head of a large island where Cube had once lived for over a year.

Close by his boyhood home, Cube built a lean-to out of pallets, ate fish, and picked up firewood on the railroad right-of-way. "I was livin' like a Buddha monk," Cube explains, staring downstream at the site of his own personal Walden. He left that paradise to work on the river as a guide, to show other people the beauty of his home river.

A few miles downstream, the large industrial city of Connelsville diverts the river into a water filtration plant. From Turtle Rock, the Youghiogheny has forty-six miles before it disappears into the Monongahela just south of Pittsburgh. This is where the wild river ends, flowing around Turtle Rock and the cobble beach.

If the Youghiogheny has a wild heart, it pulses in the waterfalls, narrow rock jams, abundant forests, and turbulent whitewater all along its length. On my journey downriver, I also found the heart of the river beating strongly in the chests of those like Cube. Before we haul our boats across the railroad tracks to my truck, the three of us sit on the bench and look out at the river. You can see that Cube loves all that flowing water coming down from West Virginia.

I follow Cube's eyes as they take in the river and watch it pass on toward Pittsburgh.

$35 MILLION RIVER

The Greek philosopher Heraclitus said you can't step in the same river twice. It's taken twenty-five hundred years, but outdoor sports entrepreneurs in Charlotte, North Carolina, are trying to prove him wrong. A $35-million, non-profit outdoor adventure park with a mile-long recirculating river at its center operates an hour up the interstate from my South Carolina hometown.

At the center of the park are two ponds between which twelve million gallons of treated Charlotte city water are pumped, creating the largest artificial whitewater recreation course in the world. Every minute 536,000 gallons of water surge down three six-foot-deep channels of varying difficulty. The water gathers in the lower pond after a twenty-one-foot loss in gradient and is sucked up once again by seven giant pumps weighing in at over twelve-thousand pounds each. After descending the river, paddlers can ride a conveyer belt 180 feet long back to the top pond. Paddlers don't ever have to leave their boats as they ascend two stories to run the artificial channels. Heraclitus be damned, the paddlers descend over and over to the bottom.

The name of the 307-acre North Carolina park on the banks of the Catawba River—the US National Whitewater Center (USNWC)—gives the place a real professional feel. At least they didn't call it Thunder River. Instead of a Disney theme-ride, the USNWC sounds more like a recreation destination—and it is—where Olympic-hopeful kayak and canoe athletes compete in North Carolina's mild four-season climate and hone their slalom skills against a manmade course challenging enough to ensure fast times in international competition.

If you're like me and have left your Walter Mitty Olympic hopes far behind, twenty-five dollars grants you as many descents as you can pack into a day. If you don't paddle a kayak or canoe, then you can sign on for a thirty-three dollar hour-and-a-half guided raft trip. You can strap on the helmet and the PFD and scream when your craft smashes through M-wave or the last rapid on the course someone named Biscuits and Gravy. You can ride the escalator back to the top and do it again until your time has expired.

Some brag that Charlotte's US Whitewater Center is one of the wonders of contemporary recreation. In its three years of operation, it has become the dream destination all the Charlotte chambers of commerce types hoped for. People come mostly for the falling water. The concrete course is a narrow trough full of real rocks anchored in placed one-by-one and augmented with artificial barriers and adjustable gates around and over which water sluices almost like a real river. Proponents of "active living" mountain bike on trails criss-cross the facility. There's a forty-six-foot high climbing wall and talk of a planned residential neighborhood next door called Whitewater Glen.

But there are also purists, whitewater fundamentalists, who are critical of the park. They say that it's turned white water into a commodity like soap or beer or tennis shoes. They call it "a ski mountain with water on it"—no better than a glorified water slide. It has, they say, a carbon footprint the size of Godzilla.

The critics are partially right. There are undeniable costs to running the longest purely recreational river in the world. There's the environmental cost of constructing something from nothing along the shores of the very real Catawba River. There's the cost of sewage, of shipping supplies and provisions for the outfitters shop, restaurant, and bar. There's beer and boats and sunscreen and humus for the California wraps. And there are those formidable energy costs. One friend reminded me that with every pulse of the M-wave a carload of West Virginia coal goes up in flames.

But there's nothing more fun, as Winnie the Pooh claimed, than "messing about in boats," and the proponents of the whitewater park claim that it's reducing the carbon footprint of a tribe that's always been known to drive hundreds of miles to spend three hours on a whitewater run.

I don't think of myself as purist, but I am old school. I cut my whitewater paddling teeth in the 1970s on ancient time-carved Southern streams with Native-American names like Chattooga, Ocoee, Nolichucky, Nantahala. In the decades since then, I've pushed my passion outward and kayaked and rafted natural rivers in over a dozen states and five other countries. How could I not be intrigued with the Charlotte park in spite of its New South industrial sheen?

Artificial white watercourses and park are nothing new. The Munich Olympics in '72 used an artificial course in Augsburg. No one thought twice about this course, still in operation. Opened over twenty years later for the '96 Atlanta Olympic games, the Ocoee whitewater course was laid out by engineers and hydrologists in the actual Ocoee river channel. The water is released from a power company lake above, flooding the new artificial rapids. It's exciting and challenging and run by commercial whitewater companies, so you can purchase a ticket and float down it in a raft.

The Nantahala Outdoor Center (NOC), one of the east's largest adventure outfitters, plans to modify the half-mile section of the Nantahala at their historic NOC outpost for free-style kayak competition.

I worked for NOC from 1983 until 1992. During that decade, I don't think it would have occurred to anyone that someday the Nantahala waterfront past the old gas station and rustic restaurant would be called a "whitewater park." To us, it was a river. We understood that the flow could be turned on and off at will up at the power plant at Lake Nantahala, but it was still a natural riverbed. If we'd been there long enough (and I had), we'd seen it rage out of its banks in flood, making the dam irrelevant.

But now the gas station turned outfitter's shop and the old restaurant have been replaced by large resort-style retail. Eighty-thousand people float down the river in rafts rented by the NOC. The company's value tops fifteen million dollars.

The numbers of "guests" though are unsteady and the corporate number crunchers are worried. Now it seems people want a destination, a place they can go and get a meal, buy a tee shirt, and watch a few trained professionals challenge a difficult course. Sutton Bacon, the CEO of the NOC, is a twenty-nine-year-old business man who understands the challenges and risks of the old-time adventure business and marketing to aging baby boomers like myself: "We want to stay relevant with our guests," Bacon said in a *Charlotte Observer* article. "They might want to watch their grandkids paddle around while they want to have an upscale meal (and stay in upscale lodging). You're out there to have fun, not be cool and look cool, but to have fun with your family."

It never occurred to me when I worked at the NOC outpost that we paddlers were already tools of empire, reliant on the power company to release water into the natural river channel of the Nantahala. We made little money at our work and NOC made even less. We were more like a small communist country, maybe called Kayakastan, in the mountains of North Carolina than a business.

It never crossed my mind that someday I would be perceived by someone twenty-five years younger as an aging baby boomer whose primary desire is to have fun, to watch, to consume, to eat a good meal, and then settle into clean sheets.

Boating has changed a lot since I worked at NOC, and so has the South. I had occasion to visit recently with Christopher

John Lane

Dickey, the son of the famed poet James Dickey, author of the novel *Deliverance*. Even though we now often associate *Deliverance* with the Chattooga River where the movie was filmed, the younger Dickey thinks about *Deliverance* in a different context. For Christopher Dickey, his father's novel and the John Boorman film made from it are time, not space specific. The novel and the film are about a slippery place—the mythic Cahulawasee, a made-up North Georgia river, but the time of the novel is crystal clear. It's the early 1960s at the end of the old agrarian South, a world in which Christopher Dickey's father came to maturity as an artist. James Dickey's first novel is one balanced between the end of the rural subsistence South and the emerging 1960s Sunbelt South. It points toward the future, to a place like the US National Whitewater Training Center, where the Old South has been replaced by a tourist-attraction-driven economy.

There is a wildness in the Old South, a violence embodied in James Dickey's mountain men, but also a beauty as seen through the wild, free-flowing river he evokes. With the fictional damming of the wild Cuhulawassee, Christopher Dickey likes to say that the South is "denatured" a little. James Dickey's mythical wild Southern river is trapped under a lake and the dam fulfills Lewis Medlock's prophecy "to push a little more power into Atlanta."

The South was the first American landscape to be denatured through plantation agriculture and later industrial logging, but it could even be argued that the South has maintained the idea of living in nature longer than other regions with more wildland. Southerners have a high percentage of hunters among its population and the persistence of "sense of place" as some sort of deep, abiding value has haunted the Southern landscape as long as it's been settled.

Since the Nashville Agrarians took their stand in the 1930s against the industrialization sweeping the South the region has been a people pulled between two minds: one, an entrepreneurial grab-all-you-can New South maybe best exemplified by Atlanta and Charlotte; the other, a sort of stay-with-the-land Wendell Berry ruralism of small communities, farms, hunting clubs, and family timber plots that looks skeptically (even threateningly) at urban and suburban sprawl and jobs reliant on a manufacturing and distribution-center world economy.

The former mind endures in literature, song, and the new local food and farmer's market movement. The latter mind is also flourishing, and it is spreading at what many see as an alarming rate. I am often one of a former mind. Though no Agrarian, my tendencies often lean toward older values, especially when it comes to land use and recreation. At every exit on Southern interstates, the ganglia of feeder roads reaches into Fast Food Nation, Lube Nation, Strip Mall Nation, and Payday Loan Nation. Concerning this mind, the South is just like anywhere else in America. It trusts in investment and abides in commerce. Harkin back to natural history and there still are some differences. A good botanist can detect something indigenous in the Southern woods. Native hardwoods persist against the onslaught of nursery stock: crape myrtles, plane trees, and Bradford pears.

Patches of the region's iconographic landscapes have endured as well against industrial logging, mining, tourism, and agriculture: coastal salt marsh, bayou, rounded Blue Ridge mountain peaks, Piedmont red clay hills, bottomland corn field, and higher up, roaring rivers bounded by laurel hells. Yet for many (most?) the iconographic Southern places, the vacation and recreation havens, have now mostly morphed through capital investment into tourist destinations: Disney World, Dollywood, Six Flags, the casino beaches of the Gulf Coast, even Pedro's industrial rest stop, South of the Border on I-95.

John Lane

As I've watched the whitewater park open from afar, I've been thinking about what my late friend Hal Rothman (western environmental historian who died in 2007) calls "the great shift from preservation to recreation." Rothman claims we're entered the "age of recreation," and that preservation is a value system that grew out of the thinking of Thoreau, Theodore Roosevelt, Muir, and it reached its height in 1964 with the passage of the Wilderness Act. This set of values ("the idea of wilderness") was all about separating "sacred space" from that space "fouled by humans," i.e. "profane space." Rothman says that Americans who matured post '64 often understand this idea of wilderness, but mostly think that use of landscape is more important than maintaining an idea. "Recreationalists," Rothman says in his last book *Playing the Odds*, have become the new conservationists.

On a sunny September day, I finally let my curiosity get the best of me and head up with Mackay Sally, a paddling buddy, to Charlotte. We drive in off the interstate, take a turn or two, and find ourselves on McCorkle Road, a narrow country lane dotted with big fenced country lots with goats and chickens in the yard.

Around the last curve of the gravel entrance drive, the US National Whitewater Center rises like a recreational Oz. There are a dozen acres of gravel parking lots on ridge above the Catawba River, and behind them the center lodge looks like something straight from Aspen or Vail, all angles, big timber, metal roof, and glass. Mackay and I follow the signs for "hard boaters" like us (canoeists and kayakers) to the signup hut near the upper pond where we pay our entrance fee and are assigned a red jersey to slip over our personal flotation devices. A few minutes later, we carry our boats to the solid curb of the pond, and entered the red clay waters of the course. It is a weekday, and there are not many people around. I paddle out and test my roll. When I pop back to the surface, I note, though the early morning air is cool, I am overdressed for the water's temperature—bathtub warm.

I take stock of what is around me, as I would upon entering a river. To my right, there are rafters getting a safety talk on a concrete beach studded with river rocks. Just to their right, water from the pond disappears down "the competition channel," the most difficult of the center's three runs. Across the pond, the pump house flushes thousands of gallons of recirculated water back into the basin from below. The sound of the pumps and the conveyor belt next to them cranking like a cannery is not so inviting. It sounds like a factory, but if I try I can hear it as something different, maybe a fair, with mechanical rides.

Mackay paddles toward one of the two easier channels on far left and I follow. The horizon line on the first "play feature" of the far left channel looks inviting, and that's where we head.

We slip through the first small channel-wide wave, and eddy on river right. We spend five minutes getting our boats under us by playing on the wave. Down at water level lost in the play, it's hard to separate the experience at Charlotte from the hydrolics of a natural river—the engineering is just that good. A wave's a wave, whether nature made it or it came out of somebody's head. It's only when I look around and see the smooth concrete walls or the people strolling past on a sidewalk with their dogs that I realize I'm not on a river.

The intensity picks up the rest of the way down and I enjoy it. We play for two hours in two artificial channels of trapped surging current, and before we leave Mackay even paddles the short, explosive "competition channel" where the Olympic boaters practice their refined craft. I watch from the lip of the concrete channel as he makes it down upright, a cork bobbing along on an engineered class-IV tumult.

My relationship to this "river" only an hour up the inter-state remains complex and lasting. I want to find fault with it, yet each time I paddle the park I like it more and more. "Think of all the carbon offset credit you could get because this river is an hour closer than the Chattooga," one friend argued unconvincingly, trying to assuage my guilt.

The folks in Charlotte aren't embarrassed about their desire to make as much money as possible off falling water, but the business model is part of what still keeps me uncomfortable. When I think about becoming a paddling regular at the whitewater center, the word *consumption* comes to mind. Nearing fifty and cast pretty solidly in my whitewater ways, should I share my remaining river time with a concrete trench?

Unlike a real river there is no headwaters, no confluence with larger rivers downstream. Downstream on this circular river is a continuous liquid state headed nowhere. On the artificial Charlotte river, there's simply start and stop when your time runs out.

Another disturbing aspect of the whitewater center for me is how the pay-per-float experience is not so far removed from a Disney World ride. On a busy Saturday or Sunday, hundreds of rafts ping-pong down the three channels and ride the escalator back to the top pond. This is the profit center of the business model. The US National Whitewater Center's hired boats are full of screaming, paddle-slapping tourists, and the guides are trained to entertain them. "Hey, Julie," one supervisor yelled at raft departing from upper pond on a recent visit, "your parole officer just called and it's ok if you check in after the run."

When I put on a wild river, I feel I'm in communion with a deep and abiding state I've always called "river time," something spanning millions of years of flow and erosion. I even say a small prayer as I snap my spray skirt in place. Up in Charlotte, it doesn't occur to me to ask permission to descend. I've had my ticket punched and pulled on the jersey that tells those working the ticket booth I've paid their fee to float their commercial river.

But because the river has been commercialized doesn't mean it's pointless to paddle in a concrete trough. Does this "denatured" river open up other possibilities? Will people who visit the Charlotte park see whitewater recreation as a possibility for their leisure dollars and then paddle down a truly wild river like the Chattooga someday? Will this contact with "nature" somehow lead to an appreciation of wild nature, and a deeper understanding of the challenges of conservation of our iconographic landscapes?

As someone who has always seen boating as a means to an end, a way of getting a little closer to the old idea of wilderness, to "sacred ground," I'll never be able to shake the feeling that when I'm on a conveyor belt headed back to the top for another run, I'm actually getting further from where my old-school paddling heart lies.

ON THE CHATTOOGA

I

It's my fiftieth birthday, and I'm floating down section III of the Chattooga River with four of my paddling friends. The Chattooga is James Dickey country and will always be associated with the poet and his 1970 novel *Deliverance*. The actual setting of Dickey's story, though, is the mythic Cahulawassee, a remote Southeastern river assembled from his experiences on several North Georgia rivers. Many scenes from the 1972 film were shot on this river, so there is a "real world" connection to this wild place. Here, in Dickey Country, it's hard to disconnect the imagined river and the real river. As we float along, I reflect, as I always do, on the blurry lines between imagination and reality.

Our plan is to float thirteen miles and camp that night back up at Sandy Ford around a fire ring I've shared with countless friends through my twenty years on this very real river. We range in age from thirty-five to seventy-eight, and between us we have more than one hundred years worth of descents into this section of the Chattooga. I guess you could call at least four of us—Watts Hudgins (thirty-five), John Pilley (seventy-eight), Alliston Reid (fifty-two), and myself— "advanced" paddlers well within our range of skill to enjoy a late October day on "the Deliverance River." Most of Dickey's canoe experience on rivers came in his thirties, and so we're mostly all well past the sort of early-middle age angst that he describes in his novel. There's little angst on this trip. It's a celebration instead. It's where, for the past decade or so, I've imagined spending my fiftieth birthday, floating my favorite river.

My fifth friend, Wes Cooler, who is fifty-two, is an expert on the river in other ways—he's been coming over here to fish since the early 1950s, and he knows the weather, wildlife, ridges and rises of this landscape much better than any of us. His watercraft of choice, a sit-on-top Perception Torrent, has drawn his dedication to the craft of paddling whitewater into question though. He confesses he's walked the banks along this section many times but has only seen it from the water once from the overblown middle tube of a black rubber raft in the early 1970s.

As we glide through Warwoman, the first rapid of consequence downstream from our Earl's Ford put-in, Wes falls off his boat in the big eddy at the rapid's top but quickly climbs back on and shoots on down through the standing waves. He's retired Army and, if anything, is not about to be undone by cold water. At the rapid's bottom, we kid him about his yellow plastic barge, though he knows enough about river kayaking today to note that all four of us "advanced" paddlers are floating in old kayaks true Chattooga paddling experts would consider out of date. All our whitewater kayaks are discontinued models from the 70s and 80s, faded plastic antiques, too long for the modern world of eight-foot kayaks known as "play boats." What's cutting edge is hard to keep up with when you get past thirty, though the passion for floating the river stays high, even if not sustained.

It's misting rain today, as I would expect from my history with the Chattooga, though the temperature is in the high 60s, strangely tropical for the smoldering end of the last week in October. Wes cites global warming as the culprit and suggests we should hogtie any politician not in agreement and leave them for the trout to nibble in an eddy. We all agree and begin a litany of the usual suspects—starting at the top. It's a few days before election day, and so it's hard to separate politics from recreation on this Wild & Scenic River. What we see around us is threatened from all sides by a marauding administration with what could be the worst environmental record since William Howard Taft. The air above us, the water below us, the forest around us—all threatened by the yard-sale mentality of George W. Bush. Or so we all think. We laugh and admit we have brought along no dissenting opinions, and we'll have to wait until we get back to civilization to find one. We are of one political mind, and the only voice we hear from the land is the river roaring its watery joy in the rapids.

I'm glad to be back on the river in my own boat with no outward responsibilities except getting safely downstream. I've spent too much time in the Chattooga watershed the last year talking and not kayaking. My own book about the Chattooga came out in April 2004, and for me, it has created many opportunities to come to the river to raft and hike with classes, talk to book groups, even once, in early September, to revisit the river with the whole Dickey clan at the close of James Dickey celebrations down the road at Clemson University— sons Christopher and Kevin and daughter Bronwen. That day we stood with our backs to Woodall Shoals and had our picture taken in the rain, the river relentlessly falling behind us. It was a sort of family photo—the three children of James Dickey, plus me, a family friend, a wife, and, of course, the river. The portrait shows a joyful group of humans who love the Chattooga and who want it to survive politically and spiritually.

Dickey's children understand how their father's memory will forever be associated with this landscape, much as Mark Twain is tied to the Mississippi. The Chattooga is an intimate landscape, unlike the Mississippi, so when the Dickey kids visited the river they expressed a desire to celebrate its wildness. For now a few newspaper articles and a picture or two will have to do.

I am grateful for all of these opportunities, though each of them has made it impossible to put my own boat in the water and commune with the river and its current. It's not quite the same to see the river, maybe stick a hand in, or wade out into an eddy. You need to enter a river to understand it, to gauge its moods and mystery. "The urge to merge," that's what literary critic and Dickey-celebration participant Casey Clabough calls James Dickey's love of rivers as expressed through *Deliverance*. I think I understand what Clabough means on days like this when I float on the Chattooga. I want to be the river, not just be on it. I carry downstream not only my lunch, my foul weather gear, but James Dickey's concept of merging.

I'd thought about merging a great deal on early mornings like this one reading Dickey's poetry on my screened porch many miles from the river. One morning I read "On the Coosawattee," his long three-part canoeing poem from the 1963 collection *Helmets*. I missed being on the river and Dickey's poem is full of river reality—how the light feels falling through fir branches, the sounds, the smells—but it's also full of angels and flight and escape from reality. It's a poem of failed entry where the speaker wants to merge with the river but is repelled first by his own imagination, then further along by the ways that a town has used the water for chicken processing, and in the poem's final section, how a retreat from the river to higher ground after a canoeing spill distances the speaker from it.

For Dickey, the world—the very real wild world—is always repelling the human ego, and maybe it's only through art we can enter it. But in that zone of possible entry—canoeing being that zone here—there is a space (art?) where the magic of entry can happen. The magic happens when you are riding into a place "that cannot be told," as Dickey describes it. The merging for Dickey is always just beyond words.

Today I'm thinking about Dickey's merging as we approach the bigger rapids where, on a bad day, something tragic could happen as it does to the speaker and his friend Braselton in the final section of "On the Coosawattee." These two canoeists survive their encounter with the rapids on the Coosa, what Dickey describes as "the leaping shore where I almost died." "On the Coosawattee" is a beginner's experience on whitewater. After a paddler learns to control his craft, he learns you cannot go successfully, as Dickey put it, "into the stone." That spill at the end of the poem has always bothered me. Would the poem even have been written by someone with a higher skill level as a paddler? Maybe James Dickey had an expert imagination, but it was trapped in the body of a novice canoeist. Maybe it's only the "beginner's mind" that allows for such merging. Merging with water and stone is what you want to get a beginning paddler past very quickly.

II.

So this question of merging continues to haunt me as we float on downstream. It's a difficult rapid like the Narrows where merging really becomes an issue for a kayaker. As I pointed out to Casey Clabough at the Dickey conference at Clemson, merging is a fine literary concept to think about, but in whitewater paddling, when you merge with the river you're dead. In a difficult rapid, a kayaker aims to get downstream upright and above the water. You hope that death is a distant factor, not a goal for transcendence. I've always found it odd that, if Clabough is right, Dickey wanted so badly to merge with water, wind, other animals. This merging seems to me a need that gets pushed further off the more intimate you become with landscapes. Commune yes, but merge? Most kayakers are happy with the thin plastic line that separates boat from water, it from us.

Wes seems the one most intent on merging today. In the eddy at the top of the rapid, he falls off the Torrent again, but he's dressed for it, shortie wetsuit, so he just laughs and crawls back up on the open cockpit and lurches the big boat back into the rapid

We make it through the Narrows without serious incident and eddy at the bottom. Looking back upstream, I'm taken once again by the spot's beauty. It's a dark primordial landscape, pure gorge. When I'm paddling down through the offset hydraulics and standing waves of the Narrows, I'm reminded of the wild country described in *Deliverance*, a haunted lonely place. What would it be to merge with such ancient stone and river channel? "The bones of the earth," another poet calls rock. There's nothing lethargic about the river here. It's all action, all scour. A nick point geologists call a waterfall, or a shoals, a place where water nicks at rock, moment by ceaseless moment, over time. It's here that a river merges with the deepest processes of geology and gravity.

On the calm water below the Narrows, I don't tell Wes of my interest in Dickey's literary themes and how his antics on the Torrent prompt me to think more about merging; instead I pay attention as Wes paddles up beside me and draws me off into the very real forest along the river's banks, explaining the threat of the aphid-like hemlock wooly analgid, its life cycle, and how the whole population of trees in the corridor could be doomed by the infestation. When I researched my book five years ago, the wooly analgid threat was real but just beginning. "In the Shendandoahs, it's killed 95 percent of the trees," Wes says. I try to imagine anew the Chattooga without its graceful dark-green hemlocks, a species lost to a foreign pest. Dickey. The Wooly Analgid. Our own history with the river. They all merge into one as we float down through shoal after shoal, the fall color brilliant around us.

III

Now, we are half-way through the trip. The Narrows and our lunch stop is behind us, I decide that I'm way overdressed for this birthday party, and so I stop to take off some gear and let the others float ahead beyond the next foggy bend. It's midday and clear. All that's left of the morning's moisture is some fog on the river, bend by bend. I stop in the shallows and climb out of the boat, strip to the waist. I'm standing in the river, working to secure my wet gear in the kayak. The current pushes against my legs and the boat, lodged against one of the river's shinbones. It's a ridge of banded gray bedrock emerging from the surface near the shore. There's a swirl of sand in the current near the bottom, and suddenly my feet disappear. I look down through the clear current of the river, but I can't see them. The sand is all the way up to my ankles.

If I stand here long enough, I will be planted deep in the Chattooga River sand, and I will have to accept a certain level of merging. I will, over time, become a human geology experiment—transportation, deposition—and the results of that experiment will be harsher than anything that could possibly happen to me as I float downstream to the next bridge where the US Forest Service take-out awaits. It's a funny thought, letting the river's current cover me completely with sand.

I realize I'm alone with the river. It's maybe only the second or third time in twenty years of paddling on the Chattooga I've been left like this. Paddling is mostly a buddy sport, even kayaking. It's a little unnerving, seeing my feet lodged deeply in sand, and the boats of my companions beyond my line of sight, somewhere on the water ahead of me beyond the next bend. The river offers the only sounds—the rapids downstream, upstream, and the creep of current along the shore.

In "Inside the River," another poem about the power of water to transform, Dickey commands, "Let flowing create / A new, inner being", and I try, thinking I understand finally what the poet means by merging. The imagination somehow holds the outer world at bay and is able to go deep "inside the river." That's why Dickey sees angels on the surface of a river and tries to mate with stones. I dip my hands in the river and pick it up, reaching for the "heart of the current," and let the river and the sand pour through my fingers. For a moment, I feel the river moving over me and even through me, "...gone / Into purposeful grains / That stream like dust / In a holy hallway." And then the moment's gone, and I'm back with the boat and my fifty-year old responsibilities—friends, poetry, Wes's story of the hemlocks dying along the shore, all downstream, waiting for me.

I turn from the river, climb back in my boat, and paddle downstream to rejoin my friends. Dickey's lesson is that life is a dance between the imagination and the forces of nature, like water and rock. So quietly the earth fills in the empty spaces.